TED, BERT AND ERNEST

Three Sons of the Empire

Edited by Sally Gaudern

Grosvenor House
Publishing Limited

This book is published by
Grosvenor House Publishing Ltd
28-30 High Street, Guildford, Surrey, GU1 3EL.
www.grosvenorhousepublishing.co.uk

A CIP record for this book
is available from the British Library

ISBN 978-1-908447-55-5

Contents

Acknowledgements

My very sincere thanks to Joyce Gordon-Walker and Jennie Naylor who provided information on Herbert Patrick (his daughter and granddaughter respectively). I also wish to thank Herbert Patrick's granddaughter, Perly Doyle and his great grandson, William Patrick, for providing photographs. Cliff Rogers generously supplied me with information and photographs of life in Rhodesia with the British South African Police. Chris Baker kindly helped with the section on Bert Patrick's war diary.

Margaret Fuller (Harold Patrick's daughter) kindly leant me Ernest Patrick's Diary and I was lucky enough to receive information, photographs and notes on the pioneers in Canada from Maxine Dobbs (Ernest Patrick's granddaughter). I would also like to thank Kate Shearman for her editorial assistance, and my daughter, Kate, for all her help with this book.

Finally, I gratefully acknowledge the use of the following books in the preparation of this volume: *Harold Falkner: More than an Arts & Crafts Architect*, Sam Osmond, (Phillimore & Co Ltd, 2003) and *Farnham in War and Peace*, W. Ewbank-Smith, (Phillimore & Co Ltd, 1983).

Introduction

Ted, Bert and Ernest are three members of my family; three men who left England in the early twentieth century to build new lives abroad – in India, Rhodesia (modern day Zimbabwe) and Canada.

Ted was witness to and part of the privileged colonial life in India which was at its zenith during his time there. Ernest went in the opposite direction across the globe, and forged a new life on a homestead with many other 'old countryers' in the cold wilderness of Canada. Bert, meanwhile, went south and dedicated himself to service, joining the police force in Rhodesia.

Between 1885 and 1903 three out of my four great-grandmothers died in childbirth. Bert Patrick was my paternal grandfather and his brother, Ernest Patrick, my great uncle. They were the two elder sons of Henry Ratcliffe Patrick of Farnham, and Alice Patrick, née Croucher, from Churt. Alice died after giving birth to her fifth child and first daughter, Alice Violet Patrick, who was born on 16th October 1903.

At the time Bert was 20 years old, and within 18 months he had sailed for a new life in Southern Rhodesia. Ernest, who was 19 at the time of her death, emigrated to Canada within six months. He never returned to England, but I was lucky enough to be lent a diary of his life, written up until his premature death in 1945. This account of his life was written by Ernest's great friend, Arthur Wheeler, who had set out with him on the great adventure in 1904. Arthur Wheeler sent the diary from Canada to Alice Violet. She had been taken in by the local midwife on her mother's death and Wheeler intended that she could know a little of her brother's life, even if she had no memories of him.

In the diary Ernest tells of the great sea journey, of walking 30 miles or more a day looking for work, of building Canadian Pacific Railroad, and the three children who were raised in a cabin measuring 14 feet by 16 feet. He was gored to death by his own bull in 1945.

Ted was married to my maternal grandfather's sister, Ciss Bateman. He wrote his own autobiography, published in 1956, which I have partly reproduced in this book. Ted went to India as editor of the *Times of India* aged 27 years, when it was a small paper, hand folded and locally distributed. By the time the paper was sold in 1946 it was the bestselling paper in Asia.

Ted's account of his life in India is full of colour and anecdote, yet to my mind he misses out an interesting fact about his newly built house in Farnham in 1927. He mentions that the house's architect was Harold Falkner, but neglects to mention that parts of the garden were designed by the celebrated garden designer, Gertrude Jekyll.

As the historian Sam Osmond comments in his book *Harold Falkner: More than an Arts & Crafts Architect*: 'In 1927 . . . he built Mavins End in Greenhill Road for a former editor of the *Times of India*. A grand house in the Wrenaissance style . . . it is especially notable for its garden which he laid out even before starting the building. While the owner was in India Falkner added a brick gazebo without even asking for authorisation . . . Falkner wrote to Gertrude Jekyll:

"I want you to design a herbaceous border for my best garden . . . as per my plan and section attached . . . The border can be made up with any kind of earth from pure sand to stiff brick earth. I have a certain amount of leaf mould and enough well rotted manure . . . I can assure you that the border will remain as designed for some years."'

I have given some of my own recollections of Ted at the end of the extracts from his autobiography.

Bert was my grandfather and I knew him well. I have slightly less fulsome documents to draw upon for my account of his life, but through his notebooks we learn of his three years with the Rhodesian police and his life after he returns to England suffering from Dengue fever.

Bert served in the First World War and by the end of the war he was Major Deputy Assistant Director of large munitions dump near Lille. He stayed in France for several years after the war engraving headstones for the fallen soldiers.

The firm of monumental masons, Patrick's, which he had formed by this time, won major contracts from the War Graves Commission including the inscription of names on the Menin Gate, the stone memorial at the Mole Zebrugge, Gallipoli cemeteries, and huge memorials in Baghdad in three different languages.

In his spare time, Bert was a keen amateur shooting enthusiast and won all competitions except one in the Bisley Championship in 1930. He was Captain of the Surrey teams for 20 years.

The lives of these three men are intriguing; they went different ways across the globe at a time when travel was very exciting and slow, and they had little idea of what lay ahead for them on arrival. They were adventurers; they knew what hard work was all about; and I hope the stories of their lives will interest others as they have interested me.

Sally Gaudern
Bentley, March 2011

TED

EDMUND PEARSON

Abridged version of Edmund Pearson's autobiography,
written in 1956

CHAPTER 1

I have had a long life, and a very active and happy one. As one grows older, one tends to look back on the past and re-live experiences which have never ceased to be vivid. In doing so, it is curious how other memories come to the surface, and suddenly one is confronted with events long since relegated to the lumber room of oblivion. For the first time for many years I have made the acquaintance of a small boy who grew into a serious and heavily moustached youth – myself when young. I remember – I remember . . . let me say that it amuses me very much to give myself up to so much remembering. This boy, this youth, eventually travelled to many parts of the world, and in the course of his journey met his full share of interesting individuals. Let this be my excuse for briefly recording his story.

My father and mother were Londoners who had settled in New Brompton, near Gillingham, Kent, where my father worked as an engineer. I was born on St Valentine's Day, 1876, the fourth of seven children, three boys and four girls. Our home life was peaceful and happy. We were not well-to-do, but on the other hand, we lacked nothing that we needed. In those days Gillingham was a quiet little place in a countryside beautiful with large orchards and farms, and I remember so well the delight of vistas of apple, pear and plum blossom against the blue skies of spring time. The orchards around Gillingham are there still and thriving, but an urban area has engulfed many of the farms and fields that I knew so well as a child, converting them into a district of little houses each crested with its television aerial.

Imagine a world without television, radio, telephones, cinemas, planes, cars and, even for that matter, electric light and electric railways. That was our world as children. I can remember the days long before the electric 'tube' came into being. As a small boy over 70 years ago I revelled in the stories of Jules Verne, but, of course, they were just 'yarns' and not to be taken seriously. But men have now flown their 'Clipper of the Clouds' and have ventured 10,000 leagues under the sea. The marvels so imaginatively described by Jules Verne, and other things more wonderful still have come to pass, and are commonplace in the existence of the average child of today.

That was our world as children and our pleasures were inevitably simple ones. Often my father would take us for long walks in the country, for ten miles or more, but the peak of pleasure was when once or twice a year, he hired a waggonette for a day's outing when my mother would, of course, accompany us.

As a boy I was enthralled to hear my father tell of a journey he made to India as a young man in about 1845. He went out on a sailing vessel starting from Southampton, travelled via the Cape, and land was not sighted from then to the day when Madras came into view. The journey took just three months. After the opening of the Suez Canal this was reduced to a month, later still to a fortnight. Then came air passages which to India, less than ten years ago, occupied three days. Today the same journey is done in less than twenty-four hours.

In the summer months of my youth my brothers and I used to enjoy ourselves very much at the reprehensible pastime known locally as 'slogging'. Why this activity should have been so called, I do not know. But as it may, our objectives were the small lanes adjoining the orchards, where, armed with long sticks hooked at the end, we would rake in the apples, pears and plums which had dropped from the trees, and so weighted down with plunder, would depart as quietly as possible. I have no doubt that we concealed this guilty pleasure from our parents. My other preoccupation with the fruits of nature was more creditable. Living in an area not only of orchards but of huge hop fields, I, with other boys in the locality, went hopping for pocket money during the school holidays, and a very healthy, happy time we had.

* * *

I first went to a little school in Gillingham run by a woman teacher whose name, I remember, was Miss Wyburn. All the classes took place in one room, the roof of which was supported by a big square beam running up from the floor.

Afterwards I attended Woodland School, a private finishing school run by a wonderful man called William Knight, who devoted himself to us from eight o'clock in the morning till seven o'clock at night. Here I got to know a boy of about my own age, ten, perhaps, who was the son of a thriving local greengrocer, and every Saturday this boy was allowed to help in the shop. How I envied him! And how happy I was when I was allowed to join him in the work. I may say that this was summer time, and the great attraction was to unload great carts of cabbages and other greens that came in from the surrounding countryside, catching them and passing them on as the men tossed them out. But I became a less enthusiastic greengrocer in winter, when the cabbages arrived stiff with ice and snow, and our little hands became frozen and chapped as we handled them. It was at this establishment, incidentally, that I was introduced to one of the great interests of my later life – horses. My friend's father kept a number of horses for his delivery rounds, and we had a wonderful time helping to feed and groom them. I really loved those horses, and perhaps it was the sympathetic understanding that I learned in that greengrocer's stables at Gillingham that helped me, later, to urge a fine horse over the jumps in Bombay and win the much-coveted All-India Jumping Championship of 1916.

I have said that our life was free from mechanical inventions, but we did have bicycles – and what bicycles – at first primitive affairs with wooden frames, wheels and tyres, and later the old penny-farthings, where one perched precariously aloft above the enormous wheel. I never owned one of these contraptions, but a friend did, and I rode it. In due course I owned all kinds of bicycles as they gradually evolved, progressing from the then solid tyre to the 'cushion' tyre and then to the early pneumatic, a huge thing capable of doing at least 3,000 to 4,000 miles!

People used to say of these bulbous and hideous pneumatics that 'they would never take on' – a remark made, I imagine, about most inventions until they have become established. In this connection, 'never take on' might have been replaced by 'never take off'. Those early pneumatic tyres were fiends to deal with in the case of a puncture. They were cemented on all around, and one had to use a solution to dissolve this, and then work away with spanners, breaking one's finger nails and one's temper in the process. It would take quite half a day to mend a puncture in an old pneumatic tyre.

Another mechanical invention that I came to own was a watch. Before the acquisition of this I sported an elaborate watch chain which led others to suppose that a watch was in fact at the end of it, but when my father actually presented me with a watch, what an excited boy I was! I remember that I consulted it at least once an hour, and I can still see the face of that old Waterbury, which cost five shillings and had to be wound every day with a separate key.

Very occasionally, my father would take us up to London and we travelled by the old London, Chatham and Dover line. In the late 1880s and early 1890s railway travel was a slow business, and our trains were invariably an hour late on this line. The third class accommodation was in open carriages with hard uncushioned seats, and the tunnels were dirty and stifling from the black smoke of the engine.

The treat of the day was a bus ride. Buses were then all horse drawn. There were no regular stopping places, and the driver would pull up whenever asked to do so. There were two seats on either side of the driver, and the great thing was to occupy one of these behind the rumps of those big strong transport horses. The recognized way of getting a seat beside the driver was to give him a penny cigar, and this my father used to do, so I was sometimes allowed to join the driver and my father would travel inside the bus, for the upstairs seats were open to the weather and were not built for comfort. I remember that at Ludgate Hill, there were always two spare horses waiting to pull the bus up the rather steep rise to St Paul's. Then they would be unharnessed, led down the hill again, and reharnessed for another journey.

The drivers were amusing characters and one was often treated to some good specimens of Cockney humour as they passed their pals on another bus. The early motor cars, which were constantly breaking down, were a favourite target for their wit. The driver of a horse bus would yell at the disconsolate chauffeur of a vehicle that just wouldn't go, 'Come on pal, jump up at the back!' or 'Where are you going tonight?', for a breakdown might mean hours of waiting.

And talking of those early cars, I remember a prosecution for speeding which took place in Farnham Magistrates' Court in about 1890. The driver of the car, an experimental one, had exceeded five miles an hour, and for 'driving a mechanical contrivance not preceded by a red flag,' he was fined 12s.

But returning to the horse buses, how well I remember the overpowering smell of horse-manure! People in these days have no idea what busy streets were like when traffic was exclusively horse-drawn. They were filthy, and though crossing-sweepers were employed, they could not succeed in keeping them clean.

In due course the embryo of the vast underground system of London came into existence. At first there were three stations only – the Bank, St Paul's and Charing Cross – and naturally it was fun to go for a trip below ground, though truth to tell, the stations were choking with foul smoke and ill-ventilated, as the trains were all run by steam.

It must have been during 1888 and 1889 that the notorious murderer 'Jack the Ripper' created a panic all over the country, because of a series of mysterious murders committed mainly in the Whitechapel district. His victims were women of the low class and so subtle were his methods that he was never discovered, though his activities extended over many months. Fear spread over the whole of the south of England especially among women, many of whom were afraid to venture out alone, especially after dark.

I remember a fright my own mother had one day when travelling in a local train. The only other occupant of the compartment was a man who, just as the train entered a tunnel, produced from his pocket a huge clasp knife. My mother was positive that here was 'Jack the Ripper' himself, and she was expecting to be attacked at any moment. She was so overcome by fear that she could not call out or move from her seat. She watched the man with the knife calmly open the huge blade. He paused, and then he merely stuck the butt end of a cigar he was smoking on to the point of the knife and continued his smoke in peace!

* * *

Those were the great days of fairs and circuses, and their arrival was a real event in the country, since there was almost no other form of entertainment. There was the annual Gillingham Fair, held outside the very old Parish Church, which was then administered by a blind vicar. Another local fair was called the Star Fair. This took place outside the Star public house, and was a pretty riotous gathering, with its swings and hurdy-gurdies.

I remember a very untoward experience which happened at the arrival of one of the circuses which regularly visited Gillingham. The big top was erected, and one of my young sisters conceived a passionate desire to see the elephants. 'Do let's go and see them, Ted,' she besought, and as we had no spare pennies, we decided to have a free peep at them from under the tents. We crept along and the first tent housed the horses, so we moved along. Then we found the elephants, and lay on our little tummies gazing in awe at these tremendous beasts, which were tethered close to the sides of the tent. But, unfortunately, while we looked up, one of the animals answered a call of nature, and my sister was only too near it. I remember her screams of horror as two small children fled homeward. I have never enquired what her reactions to elephants were in later life.

But most of our entertainment was of the homemade variety. About once a fortnight, half a dozen friends would visit us in the evening, and we would have a sing-song. Everyone, irrespective of his or her talent, had to sing a solo, and if there was a chorus, we all joined in. The songs of the day were either very sentimental or of the comic variety, and it constantly amazes me to find how I still recall so many ditties that I heard over 75 years ago, when my mother and father, our friends, and we children gathered together in the lamplight, a typical Victorian group.

In the countryside 70 and 80 years ago there still survived relics of mediaeval customs. I remember, for instance, the May Day man who paraded the streets every May Day with his attendants. The May Day man was concealed within a tall frame of wood covered with herbs, flowers and May blossom, and he and his attendants would dance outside the shops.

On Christmas Eve there were the mummers, known as the Seven Champions of Christendom. The actors were local working men, I believe, but the play they enacted was traditional and must have had a very ancient origin. The men were dressed in gaudy clothes and armed with wooden swords and they performed in the main thoroughfares. I think it probable that the story enacted was that of St George and the Dragon – or a garbled version of this – but to us small children it was just a play, rather exciting when someone got stabbed and fell to the ground; and it was very much part of Christmas.

* * *

Every day of the week came the men and women advertising their wares by singing. I remember so many of those old street cries; the man soliciting 'Old chairs to mend' in a tuneful tenor; the muffin man, the 'any old iron' and rag-and-bone man; the Hot-Cross bun man who used to sing in an alto voice, 'One a penny, two a penny, hot cross buns'; and the old fly-paper man, who wore a top hat adorned with fly papers to which adhered hundreds of flies and who ambled by in front of our curious gaze chanting a repetitive ditty, 'Catch 'em alive ho!' Another picturesque vendor was the milkman, who carried two large urns of milk which rested in a yoke on his shoulders, and called out 'Any milk?' in a high falsetto as he went from door to door. There was the cat's meat man, too, the vendor of clothes props, and many others, who all added to the colour and tunefulness of our lives.

We were always excited when the dancing bear was brought around the streets. The animal was a huge one, like a polar bear, attended by two men, both foreigners, who controlled it by a chain attached to a ring through its nose. At a word of command the bear would rise on its hind legs and shuffle around in a circle to the amusement of the onlookers who contributed pennies to a bag brought around by the second attendant.

Life was simple in those days and the price of clothing and food was low. One could get a ready-made suit for something like 15s. and a good pair of boots for under half a sovereign. The word 'sovereign' incidentally, referring to a coin, can have little meaning for the young people of today, but before the introduction of bank notes it was the usual form of currency. Changing a cheque at the bank for £50 or £100 entailed laborious counting. The coins were handed to one across the counter in a small shovel, and the quite considerable burden of shining gold that one carried away seemed much more like 'real money' than the grimy notes that are nowadays stuffed into a wallet.

We bought our milk from one of the local farms. It cost 4d. a quart, skimmed milk used for puddings only $1\frac{1}{2}$ d. a quart, and it was my job to walk the two miles to the farm before school every day to fetch it. At one of the farms, which also slaughtered its own cattle, meat was on sale all day Saturday, in the cleaned-up slaughter house. Beef cost 4d. a lb. and mutton $3^1/_2$ d. I remember that my mother used to buy as much as 30 or 40 pounds of meat at a time, which must seem incredible to the modern housewife, even though we were a fairly large family. And what appetites we boys had! Eating was encouraged for we were never allowed to leave anything on our plates, and were taught that the more we ate, the stronger we would become!

* * *

I must mention my second brother, because he provided the only upheaval and something of a tragedy, in an otherwise peaceful family life. He was a good-looking, spirited boy who used to take me swimming with him – more accurately – at thirteen he swam, and extremely well, and I, at eight years, looked on. One day he took me to the military swimming pool at Gillingham where he paid the sentry one penny for admittance. On this occasion he insisted on diving in with me on his back, and although this happened nearly 75 years ago, I still remember the awful sensation as the water closed over my head, and how I screamed out, 'Save me, take me to the shore!' Several soldiers rushed to my rescue, but my brother thought this most unnecessary and did not see why I was making such a fuss!

This brother, Bill, was clerk in the office of an old-established firm of auctioneers and valuers, and when he was not yet 20, both partners died suddenly, and the old widow of one of them handed him the business. This sudden advancement turned his head, and in fact ruined him. He neglected his work, and spent his time playing billiards, at which pastime he was extremely proficient. Then he began to drink and so badly neglected this good business that eventually it was closed down, and my brother, who had been a most promising boy and my mother's favourite child, died later in poverty while still quite a young man.

In a curious way, my brother's failings had an important effect on my own life. My father had intended me to join the Civil Service, but for some reason or other, even in my early teens I much disliked the idea. I wanted to go out into the world and be free; Government service, I felt, closed down on you, and I did not relish the idea of having about 10,000 bosses!

So in due course I joined my brother in his office, and had things been going well I might have stayed there and remained an auctioneer and surveyor to this day. But things were not going well. My brother left me in the office while he was out playing billiards or drinking, and I became weary and embarrassed at having to make excuses for him to clients who wished to discuss business. So I stuck it exactly a fortnight. Then I obtained a job with Gale and Polden, a firm of military printers and publishers established at Old Brompton, and started on the first and very formative stage of my career.

CHAPTER 2

I was now 16 years of age, and a staff apprentice, on a weekly wage of three shillings. No I doubt this remuneration sounds a little odd to anyone accustomed to the very large pay packet of the present-day teenager, but at the close of the last century, there was nothing unusual about it. Three shillings a week was the standard rate for every trade apprentice in his first year, this rising by two shillings a year, so that in his fifth and final year he earned eleven shillings a week. If this was exploitation, we did not consider it so in my day, and I was perfectly content.

Ernest Polden, the head of the firm, was a man of strong personality, tough, though in many ways a likeable character. To my great good fortune he took to me immediately, and though he drove me hard, his friendly approval of 'young Pearson' was fairly obvious.

By the terms of my apprenticeship agreement it was arranged that I should in time learn all sides of the business, but I was first established in the office to master the arts of book-keeping and correspondence. I soon realised the desirability of learning shorthand, and decided to teach myself. There was a garret at the top of our house, and having purloined a carpet, table and chair, I spent my evenings up there, in great enjoyment, studying Pitman, until I was eventually able to write at a fair speed, and passed a couple of exams proving my efficiency. Looking back, I am convinced that pegging away at shorthand proved a turning point in my career, for Ernest Polden eventually entrusted me with all his private correspondence, and he was a man of wide interests and important contacts, as the next chapter will show.

At that time, I was a quiet, industrious youth and an extremely bashful one, as far as girls were concerned. They either terrified me or left me quite indifferent. I well remember the first time I was sent to the top floor of the factory to deliver a message to the lady overseer of the stamping department. By the time I had run the gauntlet of her young ladies my face was evidently the colour of a beetroot, and the girls made such exclamations as, 'Isn't he pretty!' 'What a lovely complexion he has!' so that I slammed my message on the forewoman's table and ran for my life. The next time I was sent up with a message I actually gave one of the factory boys a penny to go up to the hated department and bring back a message while I waited below. On another occasion, during my first few months in the firm, a very pretty girl of about my own age sent a message asking if I would see her home after office hours. I hadn't the courage to reply, but the following day I received another note saying that she would wait outside the factory for me after the closing time. To avoid her, I did an extra half hour's work that evening, but she was a determined young lady and I received a similar note on the following day. Evidently I decided that there was no escape, but I well remember meeting her and seeing her home with such lack of interest that I raced her off her feet, the idea being, I suppose, that the sooner it was over, the better! Not surprisingly I never heard from her again. Then there was the awful occasion when I had to call at the retail shop run by our firm in Old Brompton. The manageress remarked that I was 'the new young man', her assistant said appreciatively, 'He's rather nice!' and a man in the shop commented loudly, 'Those blue eyes of his will get him into trouble before he's much older!' To this day I remember my embarrassment and blushes.

At 16, I naturally had done very little drinking, but a violent initiation took place soon after I had started work. In those days it was the custom when a compositor or machine-man 'came out of his time' – in other words, completed his apprenticeship – for his associates to foregather in the local pub and drink the health of the newly fledged journeyman, and this involved everyone present standing a round of drinks. On one occasion I was invited to join the party on a Saturday afternoon at the 'Two Sawyers', and though as a junior I was not expected to pay a round and was also an abstainer, I was persuaded to try a glass of port – and I evidently enjoyed it. I must have joined in many of the rounds and soon became so intoxicated that I had to be escorted home. I remember the astonishment and anger of my mother, when her teetotal son was handed over to her drunk and incapable – and how she went for those men who had led me astray. I was so ill after this incident that I could not stand the taste of port for 20 years or more!

In those days general elections were far more boisterous affairs than they are today, and there was often a rough house at meetings since feeling between the two political parties, the Liberals and the Conservatives, ran high.

On one election night in Chatham a friend and I went to see the fun. He was a naval officer who had the reputation of being the tallest man in the Navy, for he stood 6 feet 8 inches in his socks. We encountered a riotous crowd of some thousands around the principal voting booth and small paper bags of coloured powder were thrown about in all directions, blue for Conservative and red for Liberal. My friend owing to his great height, stood head and shoulders above the crowd and consequently made a good target for bags of both colours. I have never seen a man in such a mess and such a rage. The obvious thing was to get away from the crowd and make for home where it took us hours to get free of the awful powder.

* * *

Three months after I started work, the firm transferred their headquarters to Aldershot, where they had built a new and much larger factory. This was in December 1892. The question of taking me to Aldershot arose, and I was eventually offered what I considered a magnificent rise in salary, from three shillings to twenty-three shillings a week. So there I was at 17 years of age, already sprouting the moustache that was to become such a beauty by the time I was 20, looking old for my age and indeed now a fully-fledged man, earning my own living for my board and lodging. I took lodgings with a colleague in the house run by his sister. Full board cost me only fourteen shillings a week so I had the sum of nine shillings left over for clothes, general expenses and any distractions.

What did we do with ourselves in our spare time? There was certainly little enough in the way of entertainment, apart from the pubs. There was no theatre in Aldershot in those days, and the nearest thing to a music hall was a place called the 'Red White and Blue' at the back of a low-down beer house in the High Street. Admittance was not by ticket; you bought yourself a pint in the pub and were allowed to go through to the hall at the back.

This was really an extraordinary place. It was dark and dingy, with a sawdusted floor, and the audience were provided with upturned beer barrels for tables. The only actors were the pub keeper himself, Tom Arnold, and his barmaid, who was not only middle-aged, but shabby and unattractive into the bargain. Both were entirely without any kind of talent, and when the barmaid came on to sing, there were cat-calls and other rude noises from the Tommies and working men present. I remember one man calling out, 'For Gawd's sake, take it away!' but the pub keeper was not standing any nonsense. 'You b— well keep quiet or I'll have you all turned out!' he said – though in still more expressive language – and as Aldershot had no other place of entertainment, the old 'Red White and Pink', as it was popularly called, continued to attract its nightly audience and Tom Arnold and Rosie to hand out their dismally crude songs and jokes.

* * *

More attractive gatherings, because they were genuinely part of the life of the people, were Saturday night sing-songs in the local pubs. Seventy years ago ballads and music hall songs were very popular. You would hear working men singing on their way home after dark – and I am sure that in those days people sang and whistled more spontaneously than they do today. But once a week there was a regular 'do', a man and his pals trooping along to their favourite beer house about eight o'clock where they ordered pints and then sat around and sang. There was sometimes some kind of a piano, and a leader who knew the repertoire of everyone present, each having one or perhaps two songs known, as it were, to be 'his'. The leader would say 'Come along, Jim Kent, what about "Sally in our Alley"?' and, of course, Jim Kent would oblige, everyone joining lustily in the chorus.

I went to a number of sing-songs and later on, of course, to music halls, and am amazed by the extraordinary songs that I still remember, some of them suddenly reappearing in my mind after a silence, of 60 or more years, with words and music intact.

* * *

Apart from these very occasional evenings, my leisure in my early Aldershot days was devoted mainly to sport. I played cricket and football for the firm, and joined a class at an Army gymnasium under a sergeant instructor. There was also violin practise – I had started to learn as a boy, and loved it – so my time was not empty. In any case, my interest in my work was so great and I thought about it so much in working hours and out of them, that my mind was never idle and boredom was something that I simply did not understand.

Although I worked in the office, I was in constant touch with the works, and so acquired a superficial knowledge of the practical side of the business. And then one day Ernest Polden suddenly transferred me from the office to the works, not, however, in a suitably modest capacity, but as overseer of the machine department, about which I knew almost nothing! Naturally enough, the foreman was upset at this sudden promotion of a mere youngster over him, and not a knowledgeable youngster at that, but I had the sense to speak to him privately and explain that I had no intention of interfering with his authority, and was only there as a learner in order to fit me for a higher position in the firm. I promised him that if he gave me an opportunity of acquiring knowledge of the work of the machine room I would do all I could to help him. So old Tom Box was invariably helpful and we were friends.

But my troubles were not over. I had been in the works less than a week when Ernest Polden suddenly appeared and asked me a dozen and one technical questions, none of which I could answer with any accuracy. He put on an air of disgust (now, I imagine, assumed) and declared that if, when he came down the following week, I could not answer his questions, he would sack me with ignominy.

This made me think, and I determined never to be caught out again. I solved the problem artfully, if not ethically – and after all, I reasoned, Polden was being unreasonable! Since he was not a practical man, I knew that he could not know the answers to all the questions he was likely to put, so I determined to have a convincing reply for them all, right or wrong. In due course Polden appeared and fired away his questions, and I had a ready answer for each. True, most of them were guesswork and probably inaccurate, but Polden knew no better, and he congratulated me, saying that he realised that I had intelligence above the average! From then on I was his firm favourite, and as I continued to handle his private correspondence I was in constant touch with him and his activities. This was where my knowledge of shorthand was a tremendous asset.

My training took me to other departments where I was able to get some months' experience of outside work, including a daily visit to the London office. From then on, promotion was speedy. At the age of 20 I was appointed assistant works manager, a very responsible position for a young man, and it seemed probable that I would remain happily in Aldershot for a very long time.

But this was not to be, for soon after my 19th birthday Ernest Polden presented me with ten shillings to buy myself a top hat, and appointed me his unofficial private secretary in London.

CHAPTER 3

As I have already suggested, Ernest Polden was more interested in financial matters than in the technicalities of printing and publishing, and he was actively engaged in company promoting. He had already launched the Royal Palace Hotel where he lived, and had other schemes in hand. Although I was only 20, I looked far older than my years, and he relied on me absolutely and kept me constantly with him. I acted as his assistant while he floated a number of good public companies, such as the Palace Theatre, the Humber Cycle Company, the Cecil Hotel and others. Since we now inhabited the world of high finance, it was perhaps inevitable that we should become involved with that financial wizard, Ernest Tereh Hooley, who eventually proved to be one of the cleverest rogues of his day.

It was, I believe, in 1895 that Polden first met Hooley, and I remember him well, for he, Polden, and I often lunched together to discuss some new scheme that the two of them were manipulating.

Hooley was a handsome man, vivacious, with a small well-trimmed black beard and moustache. There was a mesmeric quality about him; he inspired confidence in his associates both by his tremendous self-assurance and by the seemingly impeccable social facade that he had contrived to acquire.

For by dint of being lavish in the right quarters, it later transpired, Hooley had become a member of the Carlton Club. He had been offered two safe Tory seats in Parliament, though for some reason of his own he preferred to stand for the Radical Division of Ilkeston in Derbyshire. He fancied himself as a farmer and owned one estate at Risley Hall in Nottinghamshire; another vast estate was Papworth Hall in Cambridgeshire, on which he boasted that he had spent £250,000 for alterations alone. Only the best was good enough for Hooley. When he wanted advice on the stocking of the Papworth cellars, he called in Sir Thomas Kingscote, Keeper of the Queen's Cellars, and he liked to tell visitors how he handed Sir Thomas a cheque for £12,000, as an interim payment, for wines and cigars.

But the peak of Hooley's social achievement came when he was appointed High Sheriff of Cambridgeshire and Huntingdonshire, and I was told that he cut a tremendous figure in his scarlet uniform, driving to the Assizes in a handsome carriage and four.

Hooley conducted his operations from the Midland Grand Hotel at St Pancras, where typically, he rented the whole first floor at a cost of, I believe, £300 a week. Here, within two years of his meteoric descent upon the financial and social life of London, he promoted £20 million worth of companies. Polden was associated with him in the promotion of many of these companies, some of them good honest ventures, such as Bovril, Dunlop, Schweppes and others. I was made responsible for the preparation of some of the prospectuses, for their circulation and extensive advertisement in the London financial press. Exalted names appeared on the prospectuses, such as that of Earl de la Warr, the Earl of Albemarle, the Earl of Winchilsea, and the Duke of Somerset. No wonder that confidence was inspired in the public; in almost every case the capital was oversubscribed, and I cannot recollect one failure.

At that period there were no restrictions on contained statements and claims which bore little, if any, relation to the truth. To his great concern, Polden, in due course, discovered that we had cooperated in the flotation of several entirely bogus companies. One I remember well. It was called the Siberian Gold Fields, and from information supplied by Hooley I drew up a prospectus giving details of the country and its natural features, of surveys made by qualified engineers with the certified results of tests made. The capital of £250,000 was oversubscribed, and after meeting our flotation expenses a substantial cheque was handed to Hooley. It was not until some time after that we discovered that the whole thing was a fraud. Nobody had ever been to Siberia and the names of the experts quoted were fictitious, as of course were their reports. Needless to say, this disclosure led to Polden severing his connection with Hooley at the earliest possible moment, and although entirely innocent, he was perhaps fortunate in being in no way involved in the legal proceedings that soon ensued.

But Hooley was a fascinating rascal and one could not help liking him. I knew that I liked and admired him very much, and no doubt, since I was young, I was dazzled by his success. It was said that he could get money out of the hardest and meanest man in the kingdom, and I quite believe it. On one occasion when he, Polden and I were lunching together, Hooley said that he would have to get some money from somewhere that day as his banking account was overdrawn. 'I've heard of a man in the Midlands who has plenty,' he remarked airily. 'I shall go up there this afternoon and get £10,000 out of him this evening.'

'You won't get a farthing out of that man,' said Polden. 'He's a Quaker, and very shrewd, and a miser into the bargain.'

'Will you bet me £100 that I don't get that cheque from him tonight?' asked Hooley.

The bet was duly made and next morning when we met, Hooley produced a cheque not for £10,000 but for £15,000, and claimed the £100 in addition. As was subsequently revealed, Hooley operated by means of his social contacts. He even joined churches in order to meet certain members of the congregation who were in a position to control finance, and I remember that he presented St Paul's Cathedral with a solid gold Communion Service costing many thousands of pounds in order to impress a certain member. I believe that the Cathedral still possesses it, though possibly it is not in constant use.

He entertained most lavishly, and I recall that once during our association with him he gave as many as six simultaneous luncheon parties, solving the problem of his being host at all by eating a course at each. His plea, as he sped from soup at the Savoy to fish at Claridge's was that urgent financial business required his immediate attention. No wonder his guests were impressed!

It was only a few months after Hooley had become High Sheriff and celebrated the event with a luncheon costing £200 that he filed his petition of bankruptcy. He showed debts of more than £1,500,000.

I had by now returned to my work at Aldershot, and Polden had completely severed his connection with Hooley, but naturally we shared a particular interest in the Hooley bankruptcy examination; and this turned out to be one of the greatest scandals of the day.

There was plenty of comedy at his court case, as when Hooley told how he had bought the Dunlop Company for £3 million and sold it soon after for £5 million. When asked by the Receiver of what his duty as a promoter consisted, he replied, 'A promoter buys a business and sells it again.' Hooley seemed often to be enjoying himself during his examination, and from what I knew of him, I think this was probably so. He was still the focus of attention, even though the setting had changed, and the whole business must have appealed to his strong sense of the dramatic.

The investigation showed that most of the companies promoted by Hooley were quite sound. Nevertheless, there was the Siberian Gold Field, and others, and at the close of criminal proceedings Hooley was sentenced to ten years' imprisonment. In due course he emerged and lived to a cheerful old age, in spite of one or two other sojourns 'inside'. He died in 1947.

CHAPTER 4

I had returned from London and the excitements of l'affaire
Hooley in 1895, and settled down happily in the more sober
atmosphere of Aldershot and the Works. Promotion came
quickly. After a period as assistant works manager I became, at
the age of 25, full manager of the works. Life was full of interest
and promise. My salary was, for those days, a good one, and in
due course I began to think quite seriously about the next step –
getting married – with one particular girl very much in mind.

She was Emily Bateman – 'Ciss' – a tall girl of about my own
age, whose naturalness and sense of fun quickly overcame my
lingering adolescent shyness of women. Soon we were great
friends, and went for staid walks together, as was the custom of
courting couples in those days.

Her family on both sides were farming people, linked for
generations with the traditions and growth of Aldershot, and
much respected in the locality. In addition to farming, the
Batemans were forage contractors and the firm flourishes
today. It is interesting to consider the history of places such as
Aldershot. Had it not been for the Crimean War this town, now
the foremost military centre in England, might have remained
a small village, like many of its near neighbours, but Aldershot
was turned into a hutted camp to accommodate the many
thousands of troops returning from the Crimea, and reminders
of this campaign are everywhere, in the names of streets and
barracks. In 1892 one still saw a number of the original
wooden huts, though these have long since been replaced by
brick. With the growth of the military establishment was linked
the fortunes of people who owned land in this area.

My wife's mother was a Lloyd, and one branch of this
family, owning property on what is now War Department land,

became wealthy. The property inherited by my wife's mother, however, was at the 'wrong' end of Aldershot, in Northtown, and this did not develop.

Military reviews were a great attraction at Aldershot. In the days before the introduction of mechanical transport all artillery was horse-drawn, and each of the old cavalry regiments consisted of six or seven hundred horses. The piece de resistance of a Military Review was a full gallop charge of perhaps 1,500 or 2,000 horses, their riders with drawn swords. It was a thrilling scene. After a review of the troops, cavalry, artillery and infantry, a magnificent Torchlight Tattoo took place in which, perhaps, 20,000 troops participated.

Queen Victoria would often spend a week at the Royal Pavilion, Aldershot, opposite the Cavalry Barracks; and always attended any display by the troops. I often used to see her in the early 1890s driving up the Wellington Avenue in her barouche and pair of horses, complete with attendant footmen.

The goose Hortense in 'Mrs Dale's Diary' of radio fame, reminds me of a goose that used to march up and down with the sentry at the Queen's Pavilion at Aldershot. The Queen became very interested in this goose, and when its feet got quite sore from doing sentry-go, she had them bandaged and ordered that the goose be forcibly shut up for a time to rest them!

Another memory is of balloons. Long before the days of flying we had in Aldershot the well-known Balloon Section, attached to the Royal Engineers. The aim of the experts was to invent a dirigible balloon which could be guided and controlled in some way, and a balloon expert was brought over from America, a man well-known in those days as 'Buffalo Bill' or Colonel Cody, who died in a plane accident in Huntingdon in 1913. We often saw the results of Cody's experiments in balloons and man-lifting kites, but they were not very convincing to us outsiders. When the Wright Brothers introduced the first flying machine in 1903 it put an end to all dirigible balloon experiments.

* * *

Ciss and I were married in 1900, and so began a life together which lasted happily for more than 50 years. She was very entertaining and her cheerful humour was later to break through even the formalities of Government House and amuse two successive Viceroys. But no thoughts of India had as yet entered our heads. We took a small house in Aldershot, and like any other young couple, believed that we had 'settled down'. Four years later, in 1904, I was on my way to Bombay, to take up an appointment as head of the *Times of India*, and the whole course of our lives was changed.

It had come about like this. A year before I had been offered the job of works manager on the *Times of India*, but this did not attract me and I felt I would far rather remain with my friend Ernest Polden. But when I was approached a second time it was a very different matter. To become the head of an important firm like the *Times of India*, at a salary of £1,000 a year and commission – such a prospect could not be lightly dismissed. I was still only 27 years of age, and perhaps a little excited. I hurried off to consult Ernest Polden.

Fifty years have elapsed, but have not dimmed my memory of the kindness and generosity of Ernest Polden on this occasion. He said that he could only advise me to accept the post, which held out prospects far greater than any he could offer. 'To my great regret,' he added. I asked him if, before I finally accepted, he would agree to meet Mr F. M. Coleman, the *Times of India* director who had approached me. The meeting took place, and Polden told Coleman that he had advised me to accept the post.

'But if you don't treat young Pearson well,' he said, 'I've told him that I'm keeping his job open for twelve months, and I'll pay his fare home.'

'That's all I need to know!' said Coleman. He was momentarily a little shaken when he learned that I was only 27 and not in the late 30s, as he had supposed from my appearance – the moustache was by now most impressive and this and a three-inch collar gave me a very grave appearance – but he agreed to disregard my youth in view of my character and capabilities. I was accordingly appointed and my fate sealed.

Farewell parties, presentations by the directors and factory employees and a grand smoking concert marked my departure from Gale and Polden. I still have the programme of the Smoking Concert. There were banjo and violin solos; a display of conjuring; somebody recited the 'Charge of the Light Brigade' with considerable vigour; among the songs were 'Alice, where art thou?' and we ended up with one cryptically entitled 'Ah! Ah!' – which was probably saucy, but I have forgotten it! In short it was a rousing evening, and the report of it filled several columns in that week's *Aldershot News*.

* * *

I sailed from Trieste in one of the old Austrian Lloyd Shipping Company Boats, with a contract for three years in my pocket, and a very indefinite verbal offer of a small partnership after that period. Also in my pocket was a letter authorising me to sack the then editor of the *Times of India*, one Lovat Fraser.

Before leaving London I had been introduced to Sir Thomas Bennett, the senior partner and former editor of the *Times of India*, and he had warned me that Lovat Fraser, although a very brilliant man, had for some time been causing a great deal of anxiety because of his intemperate habits. Therefore, if Fraser's conduct and neglect of his work warranted his dismissal, I was to give him a month's notice.

I was entirely new to the firm and job, and did not like the idea at all. I said I could not accept such a responsibility. Accordingly, I was supplied with a letter signed by the partners calling for Fraser's resignation, and this I was to hand to him on the first occasion of his misbehaving himself. But more of this hereafter.

The journey in 1904 took 21 days. I travelled alone, the arrangement being that my wife would join me in a year's time, (when I had shaken down to the job and found a suitable bungalow). Meanwhile I took up my abode with a family in Marine Lines.

I met Lovat Fraser, and I think our liking was mutual. I told him frankly about the letter that I had brought with me, and said I hoped I would never have to use it. He assured me that I never would.

I made a thorough tour of the works, and found the machinery antiquated. Very old flat-bed machines were in use which printed the paper in sheets. These had to be removed and folded by hand. This was all very well for a comparatively small issue, confined as it was mainly to Bombay City, but I intended that the *Times of India* should live up to its name and not remain a local paper. When I say 'intended' I suppose that no specific aim was in my mind in those early days other than that, under my management, the paper should go ahead. Later on, when I had come to know something of the history of the paper and to love the city which it served, I had a sympathetic understanding with the somewhat grandiloquent sentiments of a former editor, Robert Knight. In 1861, the paper, the name of which had undergone several mutations since its foundation in 1838, received its final baptism as the *Times of India*.

It will be seen that Knight in his civic pride was inclined to ignore the claims of Calcutta, to the somewhat ribald amusement of its citizens, and it is rather ironic that he it was who later established Calcutta's celebrated newspaper, *The Statesman*, which grew to greatness under the direction of his brothers.

Through Knight, the *Times of India* had received a national name. My task, as I envisaged it, was to transform what was still, virtually speaking, a small provincial press into a national vehicle of news. And this, from the practical point of view, meant that a bold financial policy must replace a timid and cheeseparing one. New machinery must replace the ancient flat-beds; modern methods of circulation must be built up, and the consequent increase in circulation must be supported by a sound revenue from advertising. These and other imperatives presented problem after problem to my mind in my early years in India, and all my mental energies were spent in tackling them.

The political scene was throughout a complex one, sometimes flaring into violence, but I took no part in political controversy, and have never done so. Our editors were all highly competent men, and politics was their affair not mine. Every man to his last, and mine was the practical one of building an up-to-date and efficient vehicle by means of which our staff of journalists could transmit news and views to all India, and beyond.

But before looking ahead this is, perhaps, the moment for a brief glance back at the origins of the paper, which I helped, later on, to transform.

It was founded in 1838, at a period of great commercial expansion, by a group of business firms and individuals, members of the recently formed Bombay Chamber of Commerce. Only four years before, the Company's Charter had been abolished, and trade was now free for all. Two papers already existed in the city, the *Bombay Courier* and the *Bombay Gazette*, but it was felt, and rightly, that there was room for a new and better paper representative of the views of the growing and very energetic merchant class.

The fledgling received the name of the *Bombay Times and Journal of Commerce*, and appeared biweekly. Its aim was, briefly, to publish 'the earliest possible intelligence upon all subjects of politics, science and literature,' to record news of the armed Services, supply the Mercantile community, both in India and England, with authentic commercial news, ventilate complaints relative to public and individual grievances 'in a free and independent spirit, and with strict care that the tone and language shall be such as can give personal offence to none.' Finally, as regards British and European politics a strict impartiality was aimed at, and articles were to be 'extracted from the leading organs of every political party as may present to the reader a comprehensive view of the opinions and feelings of each.'

The paper had extraordinary teething difficulties; among them, shortage of newsprint – a problem which later presented difficulty to me during the two world wars. But I personally was never faced with such a dire situation as that recorded in 1841, when the staff wrote that they were 'reduced to the necessity of patching small sheets together, of which we require ten thousand a week so as to prevent actually stopping publication.'

Nevertheless, the paper not only kept going, but increased its circulation and maintained a flourishing monthly 'overseas edition', which reached England in about 37 days. Then in 1850 the proprietors increased their capital and the *Bombay Times* appeared daily. Eleven years later, having absorbed some if it's numerous rivals, it became the *Times of India*.

It is amusing to think how primitive methods of circulation were in those days. There were no booksellers, no representatives within 500 miles, and copies to subscribers were despatched by mail. There were two large circulating libraries, which between them took one-third of the daily printing. Copies were circulated to one set of subscribers for perusal first thing in the morning; collected and delivered to a second list of names; and so on throughout the day, until the weary sheets were eventually assembled for the last time and sent up country by the night mail. I do not remember whether there was any social order of precedence in these deliveries, or whether it occasioned any heartburn to be a midday reader rather than a six o'clock one!

So this was the situation that I found at the *Times of India* when I first arrived. Antiquated machinery; obsolescent methods of circulation; a timorous financial policy; a brilliant but more than wayward editor: and much general good will.

Fraser had as his assistant editor Stanley (now Sir Stanley) Reed. Mr F. M. Coleman had travelled to India to install me, but returned after three months to England. Almost at the outset, therefore, I was in sole administrative charge, and able to strike out with my plans.

CHAPTER 5

In settling down I soon came to the conclusion that the antiquated machinery in use would have to go. But finance of that order was not available, so I turned my attention to building up the advertising and printing side of the business. The latter had been mishandled, and important contracts such as the municipal and railway ones lost; I managed to retrieve them, and other orders flowed in. Soon this department was a flourishing asset, but again, output was restricted because of the ancient machinery and old, outworn type, all of which needed to be renewed. I began by planning over some years the extension of the circulation. This meant appointing new agents all over the country within a radius of 500 miles of Bombay. These agents were to familiarise residents within their area with the *Times of India*, to push sales and, as an initial inducement they supplied the European and Indian reading public with free copies for a week. Proprietors of bookstalls were also persuaded to display the paper prominently. I daresay that a little *baksheesh* ensured that it continued to have pride of place on the stalls. Such an undertaking was inevitably a lengthy one, but in due course our men built up an efficient network of agencies. The scope of the paper had now to be broadened so that what had hitherto been essentially a white man's paper would make a greater appeal to the educated Indian; otherwise the circulation could only have risen within certain circumscribed limits.

Editorial features were gradually introduced to interest Indians as well as Europeans, and the circulation charts brought to my office week by week began to show a steady, and sometimes a spectacular rise. A daily paper is essentially a *chota hazari* one, in other words, it should be delivered to the reader at six o'clock in the morning. This eventually necessitated two night editions produced at speed to catch the night mails for early delivery in the *mofussil*, and put additional strain on the old flat-beds, clanking out their eight hundred copies an hour.

The increase in circulation of the paper inevitably bred confidence in the potential advertiser both at home and abroad. I supported this by an energetic drive, building up our advertising staff. We were soon able to increase our rates, and in a few years the revenue from advertising went up by several *lakhs*. To this increase our London office contributed, largely due to the energy and ability of our London director, W. T. Coulton.

These developments naturally occupied a number of carefully planned years, and they all tended to one conclusion: the absolute necessity for modern plant, and additional floor space in which to house it. Without this, progress was impossible. I was now merely waiting for the right moment to embark on this very major project.

Looking back I am convinced that our achievements could not have been so impressive had I not been able to secure the confidence and goodwill of the staff, both Indian and European, at all levels. In all my activities I was fortunate in having the advice and co-operation of Sir Stanley Reed, for many years Editor-in-chief of the *Times of India* and of all other newspapers published by the firm. He was a director of our company and he and I thought as one in all business matters.

I was shocked recently when I heard that the Chairman of a very important London concern was quite unknown to his local managers. This seems to me all wrong; it de-humanises business. All through my career, I made a point of getting to know our employees, and I think I must have been almost as familiar a figure to the Indian compositors and hands as was their works manager. My policy was to encourage and not to drive, for I am convinced that only by stimulating interest in a task can one obtain the best results. I remember in my early days watching a team of Indian workmen at the folding bench. The sheets as they came from the printing presses had to be folded by hand, and the men were performing this task clumsily, with several unnecessary manipulations. I sat down and showed them a better method, and this small demonstration of Time and Motion Study was received with many a grin and 'Achcha Sahib!'Soon the men took real pleasure in showing off their new skill.

There was one member of the staff who held a unique position, and with whom I came a great deal in contact. He was Naoroji Dumasia, a Parsi who joined the paper as a reporter, but who became in time one of our main sources of information about the Native States. Naoroji knew everything and everybody. The local Parsis made much of him. The Maharajahs were his friends. He developed a sort of roving commission which was difficult to define. One might, I imagine, describe him as a contact man. He had an immense admiration for the Aga Khan and wrote a long and detailed book about him. The Aga was delighted, and Naoroji became his trusted friend.

He adored me. I do not think this is an overstatement. If I wanted anything Naoroji would get it for me. Knowing that I liked Persian rugs Naoroji was always on the look-out and had only to see a beautiful specimen to begin his crafty negotiations – and there was the rug for Mr Pearson.

He could winkle printing contracts from the Maharajahs at almost any price. He could get anything out of anyone and remain their friend. In time he became a very influential man, a member of the Bombay Corporation, and representative of the National Assembly at Delhi.

Soon after I arrived in India, actually in 1905, Naoroji gave me a letter of introduction to the Aga Khan, who was then staying in Calcutta. I well remember that that interview, for having presented my letter, I was shown in and there was the Aga Khan, God to millions of his subjects, sitting on the ground in a corner very like little Jack Horner, eating his food. I sat down on a chair and from this eminence we conversed. He was

very affable to the newcomer and later I came to know him well
and liked him exceedingly.

Mention of Naoroji brings me back again to Lovat Fraser
and to an incident when we were, vulgarly speaking, in a jam,
Naoroji being instrumental in saving the situation.

Fraser had been appointed as editor of the *Times of India* in
1901, and as I have said, his career had been a most brilliant
one for he was a consummate journalist. But his drinking
habits were growing on him. More than once I took him in
hand and tried to cool him off after a bad bout, and he would
say 'You are a good friend, Pearson!' and promise to try and
mend his ways, but he never succeeded, if indeed he even tried.
Soon after I arrived I found he had absented himself from the
office for several days, and this truancy was repeated at
intervals. On one such occasion it happened that Fraser's
deputy, Stanley Reed, was also absent on an assignment up
country, and a junior assistant editor came to me in great
distress as he had no first leader for the next day's issue, and
they were ready to go to press. The poor youth was probably
terrified that he might be asked to write it himself!

Where was Fraser? Nobody seemed to know, so I asked
Naoroji who was then a junior editorial assistant, to try and find
him. Eventually he succeeded in tracing Fraser to a saloon. Our
editor was playing billiards, and he was very far from sober.

'Please, Sir, we have no first leader. Will you write something
so that I can take it back to the office? It's urgent, Sir,' pleaded
Naoroji. Fraser's reply was to tell Naoroji to get out, or he'd
throw him out.

Naoroji, however, hung on, and Fraser eventually asked his
opponent to hold up the game for a quarter of an hour, Then,
fuddled as he was, he wrote at top speed in his clear beautiful
handwriting the leader that duly appeared in the paper the
following day. It was a superb piece of work, lucid and forceful,
perhaps one of the best that he had ever written.

But this erratic behaviour obviously could not go on, and one
day I received a cable from Bennett asking: 'Have you dismissed

Fraser?' I could only conclude that reports of his conduct had been sent home privately, and I found subsequently that this was the case, for recently Fraser had misbehaved himself at a semi-official function.

So the letter that I had refrained so long from delivering had to be given to Fraser, and very indignant he was at his dismissal. But a few days after he was much consoled, for news of his forthcoming departure from the *Times of India* had leaked out in London, and one of the big newspaper proprietors cabled asking Fraser to see him as soon as he arrived in England.

Let it be added that Fraser was brilliantly successful in his subsequent career in London. As leader writer of *The Times* and later super-editor of the Harmsworth newspapers, he received the largest salary ever paid to a working journalist.

His private life, however, ended on a folly. He bought a house near Hindhead, and instructed a well-known firm to furnish it for him. When asked what sort of thing he wanted and how much he intended to spend, Fraser replied that he didn't give a damn, they were to furnish the place, that was their job, wasn't it?

So the firm proceeded to furnish his house on a £5,000 basis, but soon after the work was completed Fraser died. Nothing had been paid for. Lord Northcliffe settled his debts amounting to nearly £15,000 and the furniture went back to the store from whence it came.

CHAPTER 6

At the end of my first year in Bombay my wife and a charming girl cousin, then Bertha Welford, joined me and we took one of those large rambling bungalows of indefinite style which abound in Bombay. It was in Lands End Road, facing the sea, had a big porch with a bedroom over it, a small garden, and stabling for several horses. We three: Ciss, Bertha and I, had a delightful time.

The two girls revelled in their first experience of India. We travelled to Agra and Delhi, made trips up to the Ghats and generally enjoyed ourselves in the accepted fashion. The hot months we would spend at local hill stations, Mahableshwar, Matheran or Nasik.

Life as we knew it in India half a century ago has vanished. It has become a period piece. I have many photographs taken during those years, and remember the old days with nostalgia. The snapshots of our friends, everyone leading to a separate train of recollections; our servants, our horses and dogs, the houses we lived in and the places we visited, there they all are, a little faded now, remembered fragments of the mosaic that was my life many years ago.

The European way of living changed very little in character during my whole period in India, apart from the introduction of modern amenities such as electricity and motor cars.

Life was gay, an almost continuous round of pleasure. Servants were plentiful, and entertaining was consequently an easy affair; one simply gave an order to the butler stating the number of guests, and hey presto, a well cooked dinner, immaculately served, appeared.

What an enormous domestic staff we used to have! But since Indians kept as rigidly to their own particular type of work as they did to their caste, and the idea of a handy man or maid-of-all-work was unknown, it was unavoidable. There was that lord of creation, the butler; possibly an assistant butler; a *hamal* (the male equivalent of a housemaid) and a second *hamal*; a cook, with possibly a kitchen boy or two. A lady often kept an *ayah*, invariably so if there were children; and in the garden there was a *mali* with several coolies to help do the dirty work! Later on, one added a chauffeur to this retinue.

If one kept horses – and I usually had three or four, for my wife and I rode daily and we hunted for 20 years – there were more attendants a *syce* or groom for every horse, as well as a riding boy to exercise it if the *sahib* happened to be otherwise engaged. I may say that the horses were beautifully groomed, for after brushing, the *syces* massaged them with their hands until their coats shone like silk. The idea of using a curry comb on a horse was anathema – unthinkable. No self-respecting *syce* would have touched one. Curry combs are intended for use on brushes only, but are, sad to say, often used on the backs of horses.

To maintain this array of servants was not as ruinous as it sounds, for wages at the beginning of the century were low. One paid a personal servant Rs.10 a month (about 15 shillings) and the rest *pro rata*. Before I left India these rates had, of course, risen enormously and a good bearer could now command Rs. 60 or more a month.

We had our tea parties, dinner parties, musical evenings and picnics in plenty, but first and foremost, social life in India revolved around the Clubs.

Chief of these in Bombay was undoubtedly the Royal Yacht Club, which was something of a social Mecca. Everyone was pleased to be invited to the Yacht Club; to become a member was to have 'arrived'. It had been established many years before I went to India, and was strictly for Europeans. No Indian, not even a Maharajah, was allowed within its precincts. It was a gay and pleasant place, with a continuous round of dinners, dances, fancy dress parties and other functions, and its setting, with lawns overlooking the lovely harbour, was a romantic one. The climate must never be forgotten in any description of our life in Bombay, for all through the cold season every day was brilliant, every evening cool beneath a sky spangled with stars. After the heat of the ballroom, parties would gather on the lawn, and as the white-coated bearers moved silently from table to table, serving drinks, we chatted and watched the twinkling lights of the harbour, and felt that Bombay was a good place. During the day, too, the lawn with its tea tables and gaily coloured umbrellas was a gay scene, especially on Fridays when the mailboat came in and people entertained their friends among the new arrivals. There was a good deal of sailing too. Members used their own yachts or those belonging to the Club, and keenly contested races were held in the Harbour every Saturday. Sometimes the Governor dined at the Yacht Club, and this was a great occasion. A dinner was held there for the Prince of Wales when he made his State Visit to India in 1921.

It is difficult, and sad, to think of Bombay without its Yacht Club, but now it has gone. Built on land belonging to the Port Trust, the lease fell due in 1949 when the Trust had become Indianized, and the rent was raised so high and the Europeans were now so few in number that it had to be given up. Poetic justice? Who can say?

If a man wanted to get away from his wife he went to the Byculla Club, which was open to ladies on special occasions only. The Byculla was for *burra sahibs*; the young man's club was the Gymkhana, a great place for sport, tea and cocktail parties, and very lively altogether. Then there was the Bombay Club which catered mainly for business men. All these clubs were for Europeans only. Later, to meet a great need, Lord and Lady Willingdon founded The Willingdon Club which was open to Indians of standing as well as senior Europeans. It was an expensive club, but with its golf course, swimming pool and fine premises it was immediately successful, and I believe that it flourishes today.

Sunday was supposed to be a day of rest, but in Bombay it could better have been described as a day of sport, and I have to admit that it was mainly the Eurasians and small shopkeepers who went to Church! Our weekends were, in fact, a positive orgy of physical activities – golf, tennis, hunting, yachting, swimming, not to mention picnics to the shores of such favourite spots as Vihar Lake or the Sands at Juhu and motoring to the near hill stations.

On Sundays there was one of the bi-weekly meets of the Bombay Hunt, when we arose at five o'clock, assembled at the Jackal Club near the village of Santa Cruz, some 15 miles out of Bombay, in the dark, and moved off at 6.30 a.m. We hunted the jackal which is brother to the fox with the same brush-like tail which at the close of the run was presented to a lady follower by the Master. The Hunt was necessarily brief for after the sun had risen the scent dried up, so the excitement was over by 8.30 a.m., when we would go home to a big breakfast.

The country around Santa Cruz over which the Bombay Hunt used to run, was of a difficult nature and riders would frequently come to grief during a run. I remember on one occasion when Lord Willingdon's horse put his foot in a hole and brought him down rather badly and he was rendered unconscious. I happened to be riding quite close to him at the time and was able to assist him, and with the help of other riders we got him to the Jackal Club. He was unconscious for several hours, but recovered in a day or two. The day after the accident I received a charming note from Lady Willingdon thanking me for the help I had given. I came across this letter among my wife's treasures some years later.

Point-to-Point races were held at Santa Cruz over country which in places was dangerous. The worst patches were known as melon ground. During the rainy seasons the natives dug big holes for the cultivation of the melon and when the fruit had been gathered the holes remained and were baked hard in the blazing sun for many months. We had to school our horses to ride over this treacherous country. A good horse would become extraordinarily adept, hopping its way over the difficult patches and it was found best to let him have his head. There was a lot of jumping too, as the course was over paddy fields, separated from each other by wide mud banks. Those were great days, I won my first Point-to-Point in 1908, and half a dozen after that.

I always kept jumping horses and have acquired quite an array of silver cups for this sport, One of my cherished photos is of 'Buccaneer', a pony which was a perfect wonder and on whom I carried off the All-India Jumping Championship in 1911. Not only could 'Buccaneer' jump like a stag, but he had an angelic nature, so docile and sweet-natured that he was equally at home in the saddle or the *tum tum*, as our traps were called.

He was easily the fastest pony in Bombay and the best jumper, but what I loved most about him was his intelligent and gentle nature. He could have been trained to do almost anything. On one occasion, when the Viceroy was to visit the Australian horse stables in Bombay to see an exhibition of buck-jumping and rough riding, the boys there prevailed upon me to lend them 'Buccaneer' for the occasion. One of the men rode him up some 20 steps to a platform which had been erected, where he drank a cup of tea poured out by the Viceroy into the saucer. Then he was ridden down the 20 steps on the other side. When taken out in hand for exercise in the evening 'Buccaneer' would never pass the tennis courts until he had been given a saucer of tea, and refused it unless it was well sugared!

Mounted sports were held every week on the maidan, with many amusing events such as Bumble Puppy and other obstacle races where one wore a mask like a beekeeper's (very hot!) and armed with a stick, battled with one's opponent; or one had to whistle and chew biscuits and generally act the fool. More serious events were individual and section jumping, and I collected several further silver trophies for my cabinet as the years went by.

Bombay has a fine racecourse. Racing took place every Saturday and the course was thronged, especially for big events like the Governor's Cup. His Excellency drove in state in an elaborate carriage drawn by four superb horses, escorted by a native troop of some 20 mounted men in scarlet uniforms with patent leather boots reaching up to their thighs, and scarlet *puggarees*. They carried lances with pennants and made a brave sight, and there was always a rush to see the arrival of the Governor and his party.

I remember the beautiful pageantry of many a reception at Government House, where 500 guests, Indian and European, would congregate, the brilliant uniforms of the bejewelled Maharajahs mingling with the bright-hued gowns of the European women. Government House was comparatively small but it was most attractive, and the grounds charming and immaculately kept.

There was a swimming pool, and during the Governorship of her husband, Lady Willingdon would go down and have a dip every morning. Lady Willingdon, I may add, was a most energetic woman, and the A.D.Cs., had quite a job in keeping up with her!

Like other young men who loved riding, I joined the Bombay Light Horse. This was a gentlemen's corps organized for Home Defence, and was already in existence when I went to India. Members rode their own horses and provided their own uniforms, the Government supplying saddles and all other equipment. We paraded once a week; occasionally there were exercises across country to get the youngsters toughened up and used to riding. The corps maintained a permanent canvas camp at Santa Cruz during the winter months, and some members made it their permanent home, living a jolly *alfresco* kind of existence. Meals were available and there was a bar. The camp was, in fact, a kind of club and very well patronised.

We had moved to another house, Villa Ghita, in Peddar Road, and as this was also very roomy we let part of it off as a chummery. For the benefit of the uninitiated, a chummery was the abode, bungalow or flat, shared by several bachelors, or maybe grass widowers, because it was both cheaper and merrier than living alone. The denizens of a chummery usually had a personal servant apiece, pooled resources, and had a decidedly convivial home life!

I have a snapshot of the four who shared our chummery, and am sad to think that three of these lively young men are now dead. The fourth, B. S. Carter, served in the first war, and afterwards availed himself of the Government's offer to ex-officers of land in East Africa. His portion was a strip of land in Kenya, and when he first surveyed his inheritance he was shattered, for it appeared to be a perfectly intractable wilderness. But Carter stuck it and he became a successful farmer. He has now retired to South Africa and is one of my close friends there today.

Another young man who made good was Wilson, whom we nicknamed 'Kalyan' after Kalyan Station, for the construction of which he was entirely responsible. 'Kalyan' came to Bombay as an engineer, engaged by a private firm at a salary of Rs. 150 a month, and on the very day of his arrival was a little disconcerted to find that his chummery expenses alone would cost him at least that sum. A member of the chummery told him that his contract was an insult, and that as a qualified man, he could easily get a starting salary of Rs. 400 a month as a railway engineer. 'Kalyan' did not hesitate. He immediately offered his services to the railway, was engaged, and tore up his original contract, in spite of the anger of the people who had engaged him. He never looked back and eventually became Chief Engineer, head of the G.I.P. Railway, Chairman of the Railway Board and received a knighthood.

Looking back, what fun it all was, the sport and the parties and the picnics. Those were indeed halcyon days during the cold weather in Bombay. And then, round about May, we began to feel a little jaded. The weather was humid and oppressive, we changed our clothes and we sweated and we changed our clothes again. Even the nights were hot and sleeping out of doors gave little respite. So the ladies packed up their trunks and betook themselves to the hill stations, Matheran or Mahableshwar, or up to Simla, if their husbands could afford it, and the men remained behind to work, or perhaps wangled a spot of local leave. Then early in June the monsoon broke and Bombay settled down to three months of drenching rain, and the gay life was over till next season.

Times of India Building in Bombay

Marine Drive, Bombay looking towards
Churchgate Station

Chapter 7

My first half dozen years in India were uniformly strenuous. I was devoted to my work, and problems connected with it often revolved in my mind during my hardly less exacting hours of leisure – if physical exercise can be described as such.

The *Times of India* already vibrated with new life and vigour, it was thrusting ahead, but breakdowns in the machinery were only too frequent, and could not go on. So I went to the Bank and arranged a loan of the equivalent of £30,000 and ordered a rotary and other machines to be supplied to us from England.

Today this may not seem a very major transaction, but in the first decade of this century it represented a very considerable sum and the financial conduct of the paper had hitherto been cautious if not parsimonious.

When Sir Thomas Bennett, who was still titular head of the firm, received my report the effect on him was electrifying. To borrow such a sum was unheard of. What was the matter with the flat-bed machines anyhow? They had served him well enough. What was I thinking about! Had I taken leave of my senses?

These and similar explosive comments were contained in what is vulgarly known as a 'stinker' of a letter which he dispatched to me post haste. Then evidently he had misgivings for he went along to consult a friend of his, the then head of the now world-famous paper firm of Bowater and Sons and uncle of one of our recent Lord Mayors of London. I heard later from Mr Bowater that he advised Bennett to be thankful for having such a farseeing manager as myself in charge in Bombay. So in due course I received a chastened letter from Bennett confirming my action, and all was well.

By present-day standards our first rotary machine – the first of its kind to be installed in India – was a simple affair, but it was an enormous improvement on the then existing plant. The wearisome process of folding the paper by hand was now a thing of the past. The new machine turned out an eight-page folded paper, and could handle a circulation of some 40,000 copies.

To install it major structural alterations in the building were necessary. Two operators came out with the machine and our Indian staff mastered its intricacies extremely well. There were in fact no major hitches.

Now came our real opportunity to push the circulation, and times were opportune for there was plenty of money around. The *Times of India* under the able editorship of Sir Stanley Reed was now undoubtedly the foremost paper on the Bombay side, and it went to the buying public, so made a strong appeal to advertisers.

To cope with the increasing demand for high-class printing we installed several new flat-bed machines and also an improved and enlarged block engraving plant, we were able to show much better results. Our European staff was gradually increased and soon we had Europeans in every responsible position. As business progressed alterations and extensions to the premises had to be made, with the result that we had a fine stretch of offices which were later to be entirely air-conditioned. Even before the 1914-18 war so much had been achieved in the way of modern amenities that it is amusing to recall Sir Stanley Reed's impression of the early office when he first arrived in 1897. He recorded that he found 'no a sanitary arrangements beyond a *pot de chambre* behind a discreet screen in the editor's room and a similar receptacle for the manager; for the rest, when nature called it meant a visit to the club.'

But India is India and apt to show her hand even in the best regulated establishments.

At that time some of the editorial staff occupied living quarters above the offices, and the door leading to the verandah was usually kept open, invariably so in the hot weather. One morning, to his horror the first man up found in the centre of the doorway overhead, a huge hornet's nest. Now a sensible man keeps a respectful distance from just one hornet, but here was a mass, some two feet wide and almost as deep, seething with hornets in their thousands.

Our friend Francis Low, who was subsequently appointed editor and received a Knighthood, took a wise course and immediately consulted an expert from the Bombay Natural History Society who said that in no circumstances must the nest be disturbed or the consequences might be very serious. Fortunately, he added, hornets were of a migratory habit and if left severely alone the mass would in due course disappear. So our staff carefully avoided disturbing the nest and after a few days, to everyone's relief, the hornets moved to another abode and were seen no more.

Our offices were located at a position very near to the tumultuous life of the bazaar area, The wide street outside was a jostling mass of figures, ever colourful, ever changing like the patterns formed by a kaleidoscope. One saw all the races of India in this street. Hindus in their loin cloths or *dhotis*, Mahomedans, their shirt tails hanging outside their trousers and wearing a fez. White suited Parsees with their curious shiny black hats in the shape of a cow's hoof. Tall, handsome Pathans from the north, green-eyed and dangerous to affront. Women in vivid *saris*, dark girls of mixed races in European dress, often in a violent shade of sugar pink. Loungers spitting crimson streams of *pan* on to the pavement; cyclists dodging buffalo carts or stray cows and madly ringing their bells; beggars, often hideously maimed, uttering their whining cries for alms.

Only a short distance away was Crawford Market, pungent with the cloying sweet scent of fruit, flowers and vegetables of the East, where one could buy custard apples, tiny bananas, huge tasteless water melons with vivid crimson centres, oranges, quinces, *papai* and other fruits, and in season the delectable Afphonse mango. To this market would repair the housewife or, if her social station were such, her butler and his attendant carrying the purchases, and much haggling and gesticulating would go on in accordance with the well-known rules of the game.

Nearby too, was the area of dark little textile shops – for Bombay is and was a city of 'dark satanic mills' – and here Indian women would buy brilliant silks for their *saris*, gossamer thin and often spangled with threads of silver and gold. There were stuffs in bright hues to please the little dark girls of mixed race, and others more sober to tempt their fully European sisters, who often bought dress lengths 'dirt cheap' in the bazaar, handed them over to some little *dhirzee* squatting upon an open booth with his sewing machine, and from the cunning fingers of this bazaar dressmaker who understood nothing of western ways, would come, miraculously, a beautifully cut and finished frock or suit.

Although our European staff was increasing at a rapid rate, our workmen were all Indians. They were generally good workers and loyal, and since we endeavoured to keep above our competitors in the rate of wages paid, we invariably secured the best type of worker available. But as the cost of living increased so did our wage bills go up. We were making good profits at the time but the more we paid to the worker, the more irregular he would tend to be in his attendance, for this class of native often preferred to live from hand to mouth. Many of them were constantly in severe financial trouble. Sometimes this was the result of expenditure on a costly funeral or a daughter's wedding. Sometimes the indebtedness was due to addiction to toddy, the fierce native liquor made from the palm tree.

The Indian workman fell into debt very easily and then had recourse to the moneylender from whom he never freed himself for the rate of interest demanded was usually something in the vicinity of 30 per cent. These moneylenders were sinister beings. They could be seen outside every workshop and mill on pay-day, knowing that unless they managed to gather interest

as soon as their victims received their wages, they would get nothing.

The Indian Calendar is chequered with festival dates, and these holy days or *pujas* were observed as bank holidays by all staffs, Indian and European, just as all shared in time off at the great Christian festivals.

Among my most vivid impressions of India is the spontaneous way in which these Hindu festivals were celebrated. For instance, the day preceding a *puja* our native workmen would get busy and decorate the works with paper streamers and flags, and a happy childlike atmosphere prevailed, which one would rarely see in the more sophisticated West. The approach of each festival was welcomed in towns and villages with real joy and excitement. Sweetmeats and gifts, as well as fireworks for the festival, would be found on sale in the shops, and there seemed to be far less attempt to 'commercialise' than would be the case in Europe, where Christmas has become somewhat of a racket. In the villages almost everything required for the celebration of a *puja* was home-made, and these preparations caused almost as much excitement as the day itself.

I loved particularly the enchanting feast of *Diwali,* the Festival of Lights, when our buildings, as indeed every place where Hindus worked or lived throughout the country, twinkled with tiny lamps – oil cups in which cotton wicks burned, and the fire services were incidentally, rather more than usually busy. Diwali was celebrated by Hindus in October and symbolises the triumph of good over evil.

I remember the twinkling lights of a little village outside Bombay, with the door of every house left open so that a friend, or a stranger away from his home, could enter and share in the rejoicing. It was a pretty sight. Like our Christmas, Diwali was very much a children's festival, and the little Hindu looked forward to it with eager anticipation, knowing that he would be given sweets and toys, and that everyone would be gay and happy.

Diwali was also the time when workpeople worshipped the tools of their craft, and in our buildings one would see hammers with their handles gaily painted, or perhaps a handful of petals placed near a lathe and paper streamers adorning the machines.

In Bombay as in other towns, the shops were ablaze with lights and were gaily decorated, and the streets thronged with Hindus wearing their best clothes, all in a great state of excitement. In certain parts of India the holiday lasted for two or even three days. We, at the *Times of India,* observed a one-day holiday, and the paper was not published on the principal day.

Diwali culminated at night with firework displays. These pyrotechnics in big cities such as Bombay were on an eye-dazzling and ear-shattering scale, and were not without their toll of accidents. The whole city seemed to be floodlit. The noise from the exploding crackers and rockets was terrific.

Another interesting Hindu festival was the springtide *Holi puja,* when the countryside and villagers emerged dressed in their best white clothes to greet and embrace, and generally to wish one another well.

Spring is the time when the land and the trees and the flowers begin to renew their life and splash the countryside with a variety of colours – reds and pinks, violets and blues, whites and yellows, and the fragrant scented jasmine and other flowers perfume the air. But when *Holi* came the Hindus tried to go one better than nature in the way of colour. Armed with spray guns filled with coloured liquids, they rushed around in tremendously high spirits, squirting at friend and stranger alike. These sprays were not only used outside, but in the home as well, and many a housewife must have wished that *Holi puja* was not such a 'colourful' spectacle as she went about afterwards cleaning up the mess. We tried to keep too much *Holi* colour out of the *Times of India* office, but not always with complete success.

Lt Hannibal, Gen. N. Beiratoff, Lt. Marcoff, Russia 1912.
Lt Hannibal later visited Ted and Ciss
and stayed with them in Bombay.

Indian Rope Trick

CHAPTER 8

England is always 'home' to her sons living in the East, however long their sojourn, and when my leave came around my wife and I would hurry back to England, often by the shortest route. We usually spent much time touring the British Isles. The incredible freshness of Britain, the beauty of its villages, the dignity and interest of so many of its towns, seemed enhanced by contrast with the alien, more exotic, country which we had also come to love.

But it was on our return journeys that we indulged our *wanderlust* to the full. Instead of returning direct to Bombay we would spend a month or more in Europe, Egypt, South Africa, the U.S.A. and other places. Since neither of us accounted hardship and roughing it as 'all part of the fun', and since, in fact, we liked comfort and could afford it, we travelled in comparative luxury, and very wonderful times we had.

I am particularly glad that we visited Russia – Holy Russia of the Czars – before the revolution came and transformed it for ever. In those days we were free to come and go as we pleased, we were respected travellers, and the locals were simple and friendly.

We travelled to Russia by way of the East, calling at Port Swettenham and then Kuala Lumpur in the Malay States, where we broke our journey to see a friend on a rubber plantation in the steamy heat of the interior. From Singapore *en route* for Hong Kong and Shanghai, we went up to Canton. This place was extremely primitive, extremely picturesque, one million of its three million inhabitants living in small 'dug out' boats on the great yellow Yangtse River.

In the China seas on our way to Japan we had an alarming experience. We travelled in an old ship with a single funnel, which had apparently received many coats of paint in addition to pitch in the course of its very long existence.

One day the funnel became red hot and suddenly broke into flames. The chief engineer and his crew instantly slackened all the six or seven guys, but owing to the unequal pull on them there was a great danger of it toppling over on deck. Fortunately the fire soon burned itself out and disaster was averted, but we were left with a 'drunken' funnel which looked as though it might collapse at any moment. With this bent stack we steamed into Nagasaki, to the surprise and considerable amusement of the locals.

While in Japan, I noticed minor ways in which their customs were exactly the reverse of our own. For instance, they wore white for funerals and black for weddings; ate sweets before instead of after dinner, heated wines instead of cooling them. And how they loved seaweed and raw fish for breakfast – and *how* they bowed – the greater the respect, the deeper the bowing!

We were in Japan for a month. Then we crossed over to Vladivostock, which I remember as a filthy hole, quite a den of iniquity, and boarded a train on the Trans-Siberian railway for Moscow.

It was a tremendous journey, some 6,000 miles through incredibly varied scenery. We travelled over the great mountain ranges of the Urals, around Lake Baikal, through vast stretches of desert, comparable with the Sudan, where camels were the only form of transport, on through mighty forests of beech and fir, into lovely valleys where lilies-of-the valley grew in abundance. Here, when the train stopped, little dark-eyed children sold bunches of these lovely flowers for a small sum, and we filled our compartment with their sweetness.

We were seven days and nights on that journey, a long spell, and it was a tribute to the French who ran the train that we were not exhausted, for the food was very good and the sleeping accommodation excellent.

And so at last, we reached Moscow and found it a wonderful city. We were enthralled by the Kremlin or Citadel of Moscow, a city within a city, as it has been described. Here were a mass of splendid buildings, palaces, government offices, courts of justice, cathedrals and churches, arsenals and barracks, surrounded by a brick wall one and a quarter miles around and, almost incredible – 65 feet thick. One wonders how much Serf labour went to the construction of that formidable barrier.

One of our visits was to the famous Sparrow Hill, where Napoleon in bitterness of heart saw the smoke and flames of Moscow and knew it for the funeral pyre of all his hopes.

The road leading to Sparrow Hill, some ten miles in length, was appalling, one of the worst I have ever known, and here I got an inkling of the graft and corruption prevalent in Russia at the time.

'What a terrible road this is,' I said to our guide. 'Does it never get repaired'? A simple soul, he looked astonished.

'Sir, 200,000 roubles were spent on this road only last year,' he replied.

I made no comment, but as a result of further enquiries discovered that it was common knowledge that 50,000 roubles had vanished into the private purse of the mayor and a further 10,000 roubles had benefited the city authorities – hence the pot-holes.

Before leaving Moscow we attended a famous church to hear a performance by a women's choir of over 100 voices. They ranged from the highest alto to the deepest bass, and it was some time before I could believe that all the singers were women.

Another journey we made about this time was to Egypt, where we spent some weeks in Cairo and up the Nile. It was an interesting experience. An incident which remains in my memory of the visit was a climb to the top of the great Pyramid of Cheops we were told that it was worth the exertion for the view from the summit was wonderful.

The great Pyramid was built as a royal tomb. It has hollow chambers within holding the sarcophagi of members of the ancient royal family of Egypt. It is a wonderful, truly awe-inspiring monument covering some 13 acres. It is 450 feet high and is said to weigh some six million tons. Records show that the labour of 100,000 men over 20 years, went to the construction of this pyramid. What that toil must have meant beneath the heat of the desert sun, one can only imagine, for the mammoth stones of which it is built weigh anything from three to twenty tons. It is believed that these huge blocks were piled up by some mechanical means, but what this may have been remains a mystery. Originally, the huge stones were covered with a form of cement, but this has been destroyed by centuries of exposure, and today, there is nothing but enormous rough blocks ranging in height from two to four feet up which my friend and I jauntily prepared to climb.

After some animated bargaining with the local 'touts' we engaged six men to conduct us to the top and back again. The ascent, though strenuous, was safe enough, but by the time we reached the summit we were pretty well exhausted and were little interested in the scenery in consequence. However, we soon recovered and were amply repaid for our exertions, for the view of Cairo, rising from the desert, its domes and minarets, clear-cut against the deep blue sky, was wonderful.

Then we looked down from our eminence, and the mere thought of what lay ahead made us giddy. Only too soon we discovered that most of the stones were too high for stepping and that our guides expected us to jump from one level to another, and there seemed to be nothing to prevent one hurtling to one's doom! But our stalwarts advanced upon us, and soon we found ourselves enwrapped in huge sheets round our middles, with a man hanging on to each end, left and right, and a third man holding on to another sheet at the back. When the leader said, 'Jump!' we all jumped together to the next ledge, the height of which varied from two to four feet. It was no joke to be ordered to jump from such a height on to a very narrow ledge with nothing to break one's fall, but slowly and surely we hopped our way down to *terra firma,* and very glad we were to reach it. We were both stiff and tired for days after this experience, but it was a thrill which I would not have missed.

The recollection of one memorable climb leads to another. Many people go to see Vesuvius, which rises out of the Bay of Naples, and is constantly in a state of eruption, but the approach is by way of a small mountain railway which stops far short of the summit and beyond this the public are not permitted to climb.

Three friends and I decided that sight-seeing from a safe distance was far too tame. Being set on gazing into the jaws of hell, as it were, we managed to bribe a local man to lead us through the prohibited area.

There was no path beyond the railway terminus and the going was very hard. Moreover, we were half choked, for although we kept to the windward side, great clouds of fumes constantly blew across us, and we were half stifled in spite of the wet handkerchiefs through which we tried to breathe. One of our party felt so ill that he had to give up and stagger back to the railway. The rest of us laboured on and at last reached the summit and peered into the crater, which was belching forth great clouds of fumes and thick black smoke. In awe, timorously, we looked right over the edge and saw the bubbling, boiling lava from which, suddenly, with a great roar would burst forth mighty flames a hundred or more feet high. What vulnerable little pigmies we felt as we gazed down into this seething cavern of the earth. Then we went back, our throats sore, our eyes watering, but in our minds a scene never to be forgotten.

CHAPTER 9

When Francis Ferdinand and his wife fell at the hands of Serbian conspirators in Sarajevo on 28th June 1914, the press at home sought to reassure its public by declaring that this was an isolated episode and that the peace of Europe could be maintained. In India, remote from these international tensions and with our own brand of political problems ever pressing, this editorial soothing syrup might well have been proffered – and swallowed – without question. But this was not the case. The *Times of India* in its editorial wisdom took another, a more realistic view.

War was inevitable, our paper declared, and not only inevitable, but it would be one of long standing. The community should be prepared for at least three years of war.

In this brief record of impressions there is no place for an historical account of the war as it affected us in India, but I remember how stirred we were when, only one hour after the actual declaration of war, the Viceroy, Lord Hardinge, pledged India's total support for the common cause. There were scenes of enthusiasm, enhanced as in an upsurge of patriotic emotion the Indian Princes in turn avowed their loyalty to the King-Emperor. They implemented this magnificently by raising contingents of troops varying according to the size of the States, and soon men from all over India, peasants rallied by their rulers, were to fight with great gallantry on many fronts.

The Aga Khan, with millions of subjects, but no territorial state of his own, passionately desired to be allowed to serve as a private in an Indian contingent then on its way to France. He called on his friend, Lord Kitchener, begging to be allowed to enlist, but his sincere gesture was refused, for Kitchener knew well that this young man, near-God to his subjects and whose influence on the Muslim world was incalculable, had other and more important work to perform in view of his unique position.

And so it proved. The Aga Khan did tremendous service in rallying Indian Muslims to the common cause. He tried his utmost to keep Turkey out of the war. When he failed, with what bitterness only he could know, he was able to resolve the inevitable mental conflict in the minds of many Indian Muslims by pointing out that Turkey had not gone to War for the cause of Islam, and that the duty of Muslims was to remain, 'loyal, faithful and obedient to their temporal and secular allegiance.'

Training in the Bombay Light Horse was intensified. We paraded every day, and musketry and other courses were organised. My friend, Stanley Reed, was our colonel during the war years, and I acted as adjutant. The members were dead keen, and since they were mostly educated, intelligent men, proficiency reached a very high level. We burned with pride when a General who reviewed the Corps assured us that in no regular regiment had he seen an exercise better carried out.

We attended Riding School every day when no full parade was scheduled. Our Instructor, one Sergt. Major Coy, of the 13th Hussars, was quite a character, but very popular because of his efficiency and discipline. One morning he had a bunch of recruits in the school all going round at the walk, the trot and the canter, and at the faster pace one new recruit came off his horse. The Sergt. Major immediately shouted in a raucous voice, 'Trooper Balham, who told you to dismount, Sir?' He then, after halting the ride, went over to the trooper and said in a very quiet voice, 'Ain't hurt Sir, are you?'

I called out to him and said, 'Sergt.Major, that trooper's name is not Balham, but Clapham.' He immediately replied, 'Sorry, Sir, but I knew it was somewhere in London.'

But it wasn't easy to remain in Bombay when all Europe was a tinder box, and the Germans sweeping across the fields of

Belgium and France. Intensive training was all very well – but for what? To some of our youngsters the situation became intolerable. Weren't they just playing at soldiers while England needed every fighting man? Applications for leave to join up for active service poured in, but since the official policy was to maintain a defence force in India, all were turned down by the local G.O.C., General Knight. So a number of these boys took matters into their own hands. Some sneaked away, working as stewards on ships bound for England. Others travelled independently, via the East, or America, or by way of South Africa.

Altogether 42 men got to England surreptitiously, and every one of them joined the ranks in different regiments, and what an amazing record of gallantry was theirs! Two V.C.s, one D.S.O., thirteen M.Cs. it was an incredible achievement.

In the material sense we civilians in Bombay suffered little, if at all. There was no public rationing; in existing conditions it would have been impossible to impose this, since a Black Market would inevitably have flourished, defeating its object. There were, of course, shortages in food and goods, of butter, cheese and imported articles generally. But we were never hungry, we were not even ill-fed, and compared with the lot of the civilian population at home, often tired, cold, under-nourished and harassed in so many ways, our living conditions could be described as comfortable.

Nevertheless we were to witness, if not experience, so much suffering that life took on an edge, a reality, that many of us had never known. It also became more purposeful. This was particularly true in the case of the woman, who could not leave India for the duration of the war, and who found a more abundant life in war work and in the service of others than the mere round of social activities had previously afforded them.

Bombay was the main port of embarkation for the troops on their way to various fronts. Fit men, laughing men, Indians and Europeans and those of mixed blood, poured through the city, marching proudly to the transports which were to take them overseas. These men were handed cigarettes and other little luxuries to cheer them on their way. Only too soon we were to see what war really meant. I shall never forget the pitiful stream of casualties and the shocked and shattered survivors of the Mesopotamian campaign who began to arrive in the city, a stream soon to be swollen to a flood. The hospitals were overcrowded, the medical staffs harassed and overworked, even the minor comforts were lacking. With the increasing flow of maimed and blind it was soon found necessary to establish an institution in Byculla, loaned by the Sassoon family for their accommodation and treatment, so many arrived totally blind.

In addition to providing comforts we trained the men to use their hands, and soon they were doing carpentry, tailoring and such work, with much success. When the blind first arrived from the front they were indeed pitiful sights. Some seemed to spend most of the day in a perfectly helpless condition, crying as if heartbroken, for life to them seemed hopeless. Soon, however, they began to talk and became brighter and happier as they got to know each other. We used to take them out for walks a dozen at a time, hand in hand, and before very long they were laughing and joking together almost as though nothing were wrong.

I was one of the controlling officials of this institution, which handled many hundreds of Indians of every race, Gurkhas, Sikhs, Pathans, Maharattas, Madrassees and others, and I have never undertaken work which afforded me so much satisfaction. The Prince of Wales visited the institution during his visit to India in 1921.

Other civilian war service organisations were quickly formed, especially amongst the women, European and Indian. The lead was given by Government House. That dynamic personality, Lady Willingdon, rallied the women of Bombay of all races, classes and creeds into an organization which gave unflagging service to ameliorating the conditions of the troops and providing comforts. The energy of Lady Willingdon and her capacity for inspiring the spirit of service in others, none of us will ever forget.

One of Lady Willingdon's triumphs was a project to raise funds for her women's war service organization. This took the form of a mammoth auction sale, surely one of the liveliest and most picturesque auction sales ever to take place anywhere. I recall it most vividly, since under our 'Commander-in-Chief', Lady Willingdon, Sir Ernest Jackson, the then head of the B.B. & C.I. Railway, and I were jointly responsible for the organization.

It was a gigantic and notable sale because Lady Willingdon had addressed a personal letter of appeal to every Indian Prince and to every well-known person in every walk of life in every community, asking for contributions in cash or in kind. Naturally the response was overwhelming. Large sums of money were received. The gifts in kind included half a dozen motor cars, grand pianos, wonderful Persian rugs and carpets, furniture, jewellery and many other things of great value. The gifts created certain problems of storage, since among them were several horses, a herd of pigs, quite a few bullocks and some stags, not to mention an elephant, which eventually found a home in the Zoo in Victoria Gardens!

In all, some 10,000 items were received. Since Jackson and I were responsible for the listing of them and for writing up the catalogues we were kept busy for some months. Every morning, soon after six o'clock, we met at Government House where the gifts (other than livestock) were housed in godowns. There we worked away and were in due course greeted by Lady Willingdon, fresh and brimming over with energy as usual after her early dip in the swimming pool.

The auction sale lasted a week. With other public men I acted as one of the auctioneers, an experience which I much enjoyed. The proceeds were no less than £60,000.

In those days I was brought very much into personal contact with both Lord and Lady Willingdon, for both of whom I had a great affection. Some time after the war Lord Willingdon did me the honour of recommending me for a Knighthood, which I felt I could not in justice accept. Throughout the war period I had worked in perfect safety, had been deprived of nothing and had enjoyed the experience. Moreover, I felt rather strongly that such honours should go to those who had suffered the rigours of the war at the front and had constantly risked their lives. My refusal did much to cement my friendship with Lord Willingdon. When I, with some difficulty, explained the reasons for my decision at an interview at Government House, I was touched when he offered me his hand and said that in all his experience he had never heard of such a refusal. On the contrary, he found so many anxious to draw his attention to the public work they had done in order to receive consideration for a government honour. He added, 'Pearson, if I can ever do anything for you, please do not hesitate to tell me.' I was so overcome at his attitude that I blurted out 'And Sir, if ever you wanted my trousers, they are yours.' I immediately apologised for such an inane and unnecessary remark, but he took it as a huge joke and laughed it off. Many times afterwards my wife would jocularly refer to me as a man who refused to make his wife a lady.

I asked Lord Willingdon some years later, if he would attend the *Times of India* Centenary Dinner at Grosvenor House in Park Lane and sit on my right hand as I was taking the chair. I remember he wrote me something like this: 'Dear Pearson, on the day of your centenary dinner I find I have several engagements.' Then after a space he added, 'I have cancelled them all, I am coming to sit on your right.'

During the war years the *Times of India* made tremendous headway. Paper was very limited, but we were never short because I had had the foresight to lay in unusually large stocks. I had already arranged for a big loan from the bank which enabled us to lay in stocks covering three years' requirements. As a result, we were never short of paper, whilst our competitors had to curtail their sizes considerably, as owing to shipping difficulties the imports of paper from Scandinavia were for a time reduced to practically nil. Moreover, the price of paper more than doubled itself. Such huge supplies had to be stored, which meant hiring new godowns. Great care had to be exercised to prevent our reels being attacked by white ants, whose minute holes bored into the reels rendered them unusable because of breakages whilst running through the printing press.

By its shrewd editorials and its able reporting the *Times of India* made a name for itself. By the end of the war it had completely outgrown its provincial character and was established as one of the leading newspapers outside London.

CHAPTER 10

In some respects the war years improved life in India. People mixed more freely, the distinction of race, class and caste became, temporarily, of less significance, and existence was a more friendly affair. Moreover, since Europeans were unable to take their leave at home, many learned to know India and her people in a way they would not have done under normal circumstances. So it might be said that the war brought the peoples of the country more closely together and created a better understanding between them.

Sometimes my wife and I would spend a brief leave at one of the smaller hill stations near Bombay, affording us an opportunity of watching the life of the people around us, especially the peasants whose ways seemed not to have changed for centuries. These people were for the most part extremely poor, and their lives were short, for owing to the primitive conditions in which they lived the average span of life was, I was told, little more than 45 years. Yet to a casual observer the Indian villagers seemed to have lost none of the joy of living for they seemed to be at peace. In their habits of worship one would watch a Hindu laying a handful of petals or an offering of rice to an idol in their temples, or perhaps to a tree or even before what appeared to be just a stone. What idea lay behind such habits of worship? The simple peasant probably did not know, for the Hindu religion has deteriorated to a blind veneration of countless objects. But behind it all lay the great Hindu philosophical concept of the omnipresence and omnipotence of what they understood to be God.

We had an extraordinarily unpleasant experience in one of our expeditions upcountry. A friend had invited us to stay at his bungalow at Lanouli, a small hill station near Bombay.

We arrived one Saturday evening and our host told us that the night before he had been troubled by a number of large centipedes and snakes which had suddenly appeared from nowhere and infested the dining room. In due course the ladies went to bed and my friend and I sat alone in the dining room. After an interval of perhaps an hour a few centipedes came out from what appeared to be the crevices in the wainscoting. Then the hordes began to arrive. They varied in size from a few inches to two or three feet and were of many colours. Armed with stout canes, we attacked the creatures as they appeared and killed them, but it seemed as if the more we killed, the more they appeared in numbers. We were inundated with them and I did not like the situation at all. We knew that many of these creatures were poisonous and that a sting or a bite from one of them might prove fatal. However, there was nothing for it – kill or be killed, so we battled on for about an hour, by which time we appeared to have made an end of the invaders. Carcases lay in all directions, and we found we had killed no less than 95 of the beasts, of all shapes and sizes. My friend told me he must have killed some 50 the evening before, so in view of what the morrow might bring we decided to return to Bombay the very next day!

I confess that I do not like snakes. They are rarely seen in Bombay City itself, but one day while my wife and I were having tea in the garden with the Commissioner of Police and his wife Sir Patrick and Lady Kelly, a large snake emerged from the rocks nearby. We kept calm, but it was not a pleasant experience as the snake – all six feet long – made its way in our direction and passed within inches of us. It called for great self control, but no harm came to us as we remained perfectly still and quiet and eventually the snake glided away to its home in the rocks.

I once witnessed an incredible demonstration of fire-walking by a very old Burmese. He was not the sole performer – the remarkable thing was that he enabled others to perform the feat. We were with Sir Patrick Kelly, the then Commissioner of Police in Bombay, and there were present many other Europeans as well as a large number of Indians. A trench, some thirty feet in length, about ten feet in width and two feet in depth, had been prepared and filled with dry logs of wood set on fire, the embers of which were already red hot.

The *fakir* announced that he possessed such control of fire that he would, with bare feet and bare legs up to his thighs, walk slowly through the length of the trench through the fire which was almost at white heat, without hurt or injury of any kind. First he sent his servant through, following immediately himself. He then invited any of us to follow, assuring us that we could go through with bare feet and legs without the least harm. He explained that such was his control over the fire that so long as his arms were raised above his head there was no risk whatever, but as soon as he felt the power leaving him, he would drop his arms as a signal that everybody in the trench should immediately jump out or they might be seriously burned.

Some 50 people, Europeans and Indians, men and women, took off their shoes and walked through the fire with bare feet and legs experiencing no feeling of injury whatever. Among them were ladies known to me whose silk stockings showed not the least sign of injury from the fire. All were anticipating a signal from the *fakir*, and at length it came. After a time he suddenly dropped his arms and everybody jumped for it. Those who were anticipating the signal escaped without the slightest injury. Those who delayed said afterwards that although they felt the heat, they also escaped without being even slightly burned. The *fakir* explained that as there were a large number of people going through the fire his power was limited, and he could not protect them all. I can offer no explanation of this extraordinary display. The fire was certainly genuine for its heat was so great that our party could not approach within yards of it. A friend attributed the phenomenon to mass mesmerism, but whether this was so or not, we shall never know.

I first met the Aga Khan in Calcutta in 1905. Subsequently we saw much of each other and I have always entertained a warm regard for him. He is 'of course' the spiritual head of a section of the Mahomedan brotherhood which has always been very widespread in India and in East Africa. All sects are now included in the State of Pakistan. He was always a popular figure in Bombay, a very pleasant companion and a good sportsman. I occasionally played golf with him at the Willingdon Club. Since his followers claim that he is the direct descendant of the Prophet Mohamed, they maintain that he is it man incapable of sin.

There is an amusing story which illustrates this belief. A non-Muslim in conversation with an orthodox follower was criticising His Highness's mild indulgence in intoxicating liquors as being directly opposed to the teachings of Islam. Said the Muslim, 'Yes, my friend, but what you do not understand is that the alcohol turns to water on touching the Aga Khan's lips.'

The critic rejoined, 'Well, the same thing happens to me, only it takes longer.'

On more than one occasion I met Mahatma Gandhi and his successor Jawaharlal Nehru, the present ruler of India. In the course of talks with Gandhi I may not have agreed entirely with his arguments, but I was nevertheless greatly impressed with his personality and his wonderful character.

He was a man of very simple habits, an ascetic, living in the same style as the humblest of his followers, and devoting his life to helping those who could not help themselves. His influence was incalculable. Whenever he visited Bombay he would be met by thousands, and so vast were the crowds that extra police had to be called in to assist in controlling the traffic. I remember a tremendous occasion when Gandhi spoke on the Bombay *Maidan* to a gathering which must have numbered at least one hundred thousand.

Nehru was his ardent disciple. He was at one time a confirmed Communist and served several terms of imprisonment for acts of civil disobedience. A brief visit to Moscow led him to renounce Communism, and when the Indian Government came into power he was at once selected as a man to control the new regime. I liked Nehru for his integrity and his ability, and consider that today he is doing a great work for his country in spite of what have been described as unusual methods.

Perhaps the majority of my non-European friends were among the Parsees. They included many of the well-known influential men in Bombay City. They were a very enlightened community and we often dined with them. The Parsees came to India some 700 years ago when they were driven out of Persia after religious persecution by the Mahomedan invaders. Of their total strength of about 100,000 in India, half of them resided in Bombay City. Generally speaking they were a very sophisticated community and numbered among them many merchants, financiers and leaders of industry. Although very westernised, the older members of the community with whom I came into contact were usually orthodox Zoroastrians, or Fire Worshippers, and woe betide a young emancipated Parsee who attempted to light a cigarette in their presence – smoking just wasn't done.

CHAPTER 11

A major event after the 1914-18 War was the visit of the Prince of Wales to India in 1921. Outwardly this was one of those outstanding displays of pageantry in which the British excel, a marvel of splendour, dignity and timing. The actual impact of the royal visit on both Europeans and Indians was far more complex.

At sunrise on 17th November, we heard the guns of the East Indies Squadron and of the French cruiser *d'Este* salute the arrival of *H.M.S. Renown* in Bombay Harbour. At ten o'clock the Prince's Barge swung alongside *Apollo Bunder*, where he was greeted by the Viceroy, Lord Reading, and by Sir George Lloyd, Governor of the Bombay Presidency, behind whom, in glittering array of silken uniforms and bejewelled turbans, were the Indian Princes who were to attend the Prince on his tour.

I remember the scene most vividly. The Prince passed through the famous Gateway of India to a pavilion which had been specially erected for the occasion, an Arabian Nights affair with gilt minarets on which the sun sparkled, and a central dome, emblazoned with the Royal Coat of Arms. In the presence of several thousand dignitaries, both European and Indian, the Prince read a message from his father, the King Emperor. Then, in a horse-drawn carriage, with an escort of scarlet Cavalry, he drove in state through five miles of beflagged streets to Government House, at Malabar Point.

It was an anxious time for all officialdom responsible for the safety of the Prince, for in protest at the royal visit Gandhi had called on his followers to stage a *hartal* or strike on the day of his arrival, and ordered them to remain indoors. Many thousands disobeyed his injunction and the royal procession was in no sense a 'frost', for the streets were well-lined with a hand-clapping, excited crowd of natives. But violence was afoot in the bazaars, and as so often this took the form of communal rioting. The police had to fire on the mob to restore order, and behind all the pomp which unfolded with such certainty of timing during the Prince's three-day visit to Bombay, the air was electric with tension.

For those nearest the person of the Prince, anxiety was often acute, for he was in some ways little more than an over-grown boy, wilful and anxious to have his own way. Courageous and by nature unconventional, he wanted to see behind and beyond the panoply of officialdom presented to him. The few words of his own forming a postscript to the stately message from his father, the King-Emperor, seemed to express this.

'I want to know you, and I want you to know me,' said the Prince, and it was clear that his words were intended to extend to those Indians who were not present in that dazzling pavilion; he wanted to know and be known by the masses, the ordinary men and women of India.

It was a laudable wish and a brave one, but in the existing state of affairs it was small wonder that those whose duty it was to protect the Prince were often troubled. He would, for instance, get up early in the morning and try to go down to the bazaars. But the bazaars were in an uproar and he had to be restrained from doing so. During his stay in Bombay the Prince witnessed a naval and military pageant on the *Maidan*. On this occasion also he caused anxiety, for he refused to leave by the route arranged for him which was lined with 'people of consequence', (who consequently felt extremely aggrieved) and made his way out through a seething crowd of Indians – the people he wanted to get to know – a gesture which, it happens, turned out well, judging by the hullabaloo of applause from the natives – but then it might not have turned out well, for violence was in the air.

In other ways the Prince shocked officialdom. Perhaps it was his youthfulness and a reaction against his upbringing, but the rigid protocol or order of precedence which was observed at every function bored him, and at times his boredom was apparent. I remember that we entertained him to a dance at the Byculla Club. He was, needless to say, expected to lead off with the wife of the President of the Club. Instead, he pointed out a pretty girl, a social 'nobody', and elected to dance first with her. It was all very natural perhaps, but it did not go down very well – and certainly not with the wife of the President!

Given a horse, the Prince was happy. He loved a game of polo, he loved the races, he was a good and dashing rider, never averse to taking risks. I suppose he was, in fact, a very normal youngster anxious to enjoy himself, and prove his courage in his own right; to be a figurehead, the Prince of Wales, a kind of conventional dummy, irked him. His character led him to break away from tradition, as his later story showed. In India, the seeds of what was to develop had already germinated.

The Prince made an extended tour of the native states, and at Gwalior, as the guest of the Maharaja Scindia, I took part in the incredible splendour of the ceremonies which marked his visit. The procession in which the Prince made his state entry was said to be one of the finest spectacles in the Indian tour. It was indeed breathtaking in its magnificence, and because such a thing will never be seen again, I will describe in it some detail.

The procession began at Gwalior station, where the Prince alighted to find a tremendous elephant, wondrously bedizened, kneeling and surrounded in a semi-circle by eighteen other state elephants, one of which, incidentally, was to be my mount. The Prince and the Maharaja climbed a ladder and installed themselves in a gold two-seated *howdah*, and then, to a flourish of trumpets, the great beast rose to his feet.

The appearance of that elephant was quite extraordinary. He was said to be of immense age, 100 years or more, and he had been so worked on that he was a carnival in himself, a splendid figure and yet, perhaps, a little sad, too. His face had been painted a deep yellow, his eyes rimmed with red paint, his body plastered with gold paint. Beneath the *howdah* he was draped in a vast mantle of crimson silk, on his legs were massive silver anklets, and bells jingled with every movement of his vast body.

The other elephants followed in couples. Six were silvered all over and bore silver *howdahs*; the others were mainly light blue with brilliantly decorated side cloths. The head and trunks of the elephants were painted with formalistic designs in vivid colours.

In the vanguard of the procession were other elephants carrying great kettledrums; still others with crimson standards carried by Indian officers; led horses in gorgeous trappings with jewelled aigrettes nodding behind their ears; processions of cavalry, guns, foot soldiers; enormous palanquins – one, I remember, plated with gold – borne by staggering bands of Palace servants; state carriages – I do not know what else, but the total effect in my mind is of a tremendous medley of flashing colour, of glitter, of the strident din of trumpet and kettledrum, and the roar of applauding people, of a barbaric splendour unequalled, unwinding under the brilliant blue of the Indian sky.

The following day the Prince reviewed the State forces of Gwalior, a sizeable and highly efficient army of some 5,000 men in khaki uniforms with white leggings and coloured puggarees. The scene was not without its light relief, for the two small children of the Maharaja, George, the Heir-Apparent and his sister, Mary, appeared dressed as miniature soldiers fully equipped, and marched as privates with the infantry battalion. The Prince enjoyed this pleasant little joke no less than the proud father, but the review was a fairly lengthy business, and as the Maharaja told me some time later, his royal guest appeared to be getting a bit restless. The Maharaja was a youngish man and a very good sport. He understood. Turning to the Prince he whispered, conspiratorially, 'Your Highness, do you find this interesting?' Receiving a polite but non-committal answer, he said, 'How about a game of Polo?' The Prince's face lit up and, without more ado the two most important people of the show crept away like thieves to the polo ground about a mile away, and there disported themselves in a manner more congenial to them both.

During his two-day stay in Gwalior the Prince took part in a tiger shoot. It was essential that he should get his tiger, and, in fact, eight tigers were shot by the Royal Party. But how to ensure the tigers were there? Tremendous preparations had, of course, been set afoot for weeks preceding his visit. Some 1,000 men had been stationed in the jungle, making a tremendous clatter and urging the beasts towards a certain position. Having got them into an area of perhaps a quarter of a square mile, the men remained on duty day and night to see that no tiger made its escape before the time of the shoot. The Prince of Wales and his party were seated in *machans* erected in trees; and when the Prince was ready the tiger was urged somewhere within the vicinity of the tree – a not too difficult target. Such an arrangement sounds neither very exciting nor very sporting, but it was no special innovation for the benefit of the Prince of Wales. An Indian Prince would lay on a shoot of this kind for any important person, for it would have been considered unthinkable not to produce a tiger for an august guest.

My wife and I were frequently guests of the Maharajah of Gwalior on occasions when important visitors such as Viceroys were entertained. On such occasions he would have a miniature railway running round the dining table controlled by an electric button. The two carriages contained after-dinner wines and cigars. He would ask one of his visitors at the other end of the table whether he would take a glass of port or a cigar with him, and then send the little railway forward, stopping it just in front of his guest. Just as the latter was about to take a smoke the Maharajah would delight in starting the railway and running it past the guest. His Highness thought this a great joke and would laugh heartily at the surprise of the assembled company.

My wife was always popular for her cheerful disposition and her ready wit. She had a fund of humorous stories so was in great demand at dinner parties. I remember we were once invited to stay with the Maharajah of Bhopal on the occasion of the visit of the Viceroy, Lord Reading, and Lady Reading. As was the custom, distinguished visitors were invited after dinner to a private room there to meet a few of the other principal guests of the evening. My wife was asked to speak to the Viceroy and was shown into his room for a ten-minute talk. She was warned that she should not exceed the allotted time as there were other guests to follow. After ten minutes the A.D.C. looked at his watch and again at fifteen minutes. At twenty minutes he seemed to be getting anxious, and when half an hour went by he was positively agitated. Finally my wife appeared with a smile on her face.

The A.D.C. said, 'Mrs Pearson, you have been with His Excellency just twenty minutes too long. What have you been talking about?'

She replied, in her usual humorous way, 'You are just two years too young to understand!' The A.D.C. pretended to be amused, but he was in reality, not a little annoyed.

My wife added, 'His Excellency asked me to say that he cannot receive any other guests as he is going to bed.'

She told me afterwards that she had started telling H.E. funny stories, and he would not let her finish, so amused was he, so her time allowance was greatly exceeded although she had tried hard several times to get away. He said eventually, 'Mrs Pearson, this is the most amusing half hour I have spent since coming to India, and I am not going to let it be spoilt by talking to anyone else!'

On another occasion that I visited Dharampur I was, literally, almost overcome by the liberality of the Maharana.

First of all there was a night shoot. A *machan* had been erected and an old *shikari* or huntsman placed at my service. On the ground below there was a small platform some three feet high on which was tied a small goat, intended as a bait to induce the panther to come out and attack. As it was dark the *shikari* was armed with an electric torch. The idea was that as soon as Master Panther came round to inspect the kill, the torch would be turned on him and I would fire before he harmed the little goat. All worked out according to plan. The panther crept alongside the platform ready to spring on his prey, I fired at his upturned face pin-pointed by the light, and rolled him over at the first shot.

It must have been near 11 o'clock when I arrived back at the Guest House, and I was very tired for I had been out and shot another panther in the morning. Bed was what I dearly wanted, but a late dinner had been arranged with His Highness, and I had to wade through six courses, knowing that he would have felt hurt if I had refused the meal. I had grossly overeaten, I was dead beat, I longed to lie down and go to sleep, but there was much more to endure. As the last of the English meal was borne away the Maharana announced that his dinner, an Indian preparation, would now be served. I mildly protested that I could not eat another thing, but it was no use.

'Mr Pearson, I have joined you in *your* dinner because you are my guest,' said the Maharana. 'If you do not now join me in mine I cannot eat myself, for it would be the height of rudeness for me to eat alone in the presence of my guest.'

There was nothing for it, I had to swallow curry and rice and a number of other Indian dishes, and to this day I do not know how I managed it. And now bed, I thought. Bed at last! But no, H.H. then announced that he had arranged an Indian entertainment on the verandah for my special benefit, and I had to sit down and watch a display of Indian dancing and juggling, which would have interested me if I had felt a little less weary.

One particular item I remember, the first on the programme. It was an effort on the bagpipes by an Indian in Highland costume, who marched up and down the verandah playing just one line from a Scottish air! After ten minutes of this I began to feel frantic, when to my intense relief the Maharana turned to me and said, 'Are you enjoying the bagpipes?'

My reply was a decided negative, to which he said, 'I am so glad to hear that because I myself hate the noise, but I thought it might please you!' Hospitality could go no further.

His Highness once asked me up for a shoot shortly before I was due to sail for England, and my timetable was so crowded that I had to write asking to be excused. Immediately came a telegram with the words, 'You have promised.' So there was nothing for it but to take the first train up to Dharampur.

I was very fond indeed of the Maharana, who was one of the kindest men I have ever met. He visited me at my home in Farnham, Surrey, a few years after this last shoot, and seemed to be charmed with my house and garden and with my collection of Indian pictures and *objets d'art*.

The Maharana is now dead, and I hope happier than he was in his last years. I have, in my study, a very attractive silver ornament, beautifully embossed, with an inscription which reads: *To E. G. Pearson, Esq., as a token of friendship and regard from Maharana Shri Vijayadevji Rana Raja Sahib of Dharampur,*' with the date 3rd April 1927. I value it greatly as the gift of a most lovable and generous man.

Ciss on Melody

Ted on Buchaneer

Ted and family in Portofino 1935. RMS 'Atlantis' cruise.

Ted, Ciss, Edie, Peggy and Mollie Bateman,
in Portofino 1935

Ted and family in Tangiers 1935

Mavins End, Greenhill Road, Farnham.

CHAPTER 12

After my first 20 years in India I found it necessary for business and other purposes to spend some months every year in England – a pleasant arrangement, as it meant enjoying the best of both worlds, an English summer, and an Indian winter, if winter can be said to describe the perfect climate with a daytime temperature of 75 or 80 degrees, and nights some 10 degrees lower, of the cool season in Bombay.

Hitherto my wife and I had spent our leaves either with friends or in hotels, and as we travelled a great deal we had not missed a permanent home. But now, with so many months yearly in England ahead of us, we needed one. So we began looking around for the ideal house on the perfect site, and since this was rather a tall order we could not find it. Accordingly we decided to build our own house, and in 1925 I bought a lovely five-acre plot of sloping land at Farnham in Surrey, near enough to Aldershot for us to feel very much at home.

The construction of that house and garden was a great interest to us both. I arranged with a local architect for the land to be developed first, so that by the time the house was built, we should have a comparatively mature garden. This was a big job, as it entailed the building of terraces and a good deal of excavation work. The garden took three years, the house a further year to complete, and both were beautiful.

Our architect, Mr H. F. Falkner of Farnham, had vision. From the house, which is dignified, well-proportioned and restful, a flight of steps leads to a terrace where long pools reflect the brilliant colours of flower beds and are bright with water lilies and the glint of goldfish. There are sloping lawns, wide flower beds, banks of rhododendron and many other flowering shrubs, and near the house is a 'wild' corner – the original land with the pine trees and heath so typical of Surrey. Occasionally I throw the garden open to the public, and it appears to give our visitors much pleasure. I can hardly pay a greater tribute to the architect than by saying that there is no detail in either house or garden that I would wish to change in any way.

We filled our home with beautiful things. During my years in India I had collected some 60 Persian carpets and rugs. Among them is an Ardebil rug, one of only two copies, I believe, of the famous sixteenth-century floral carpet exhibited in the Victoria and Albert Museum. I was told that the value of my carpet is about £1,000. To check this, but not with any intention of selling, I once put it up for auction but pulled out when the dealers bid up to £500. The Ardebil is a woollen rug, but the texture is almost as fine as silk, and the colours glow.

I have a four-fold Japanese screen, in which tiny silken stitches go to form a series of beautiful landscapes – an oriental 'tapestry' of the greatest delicacy. Some years ago the monsoon damp rotted some parts of the screen, and I asked the Gentlewomen's Needlework Association in London if they would undertake to repair it. In agreeing to do so, they wrote me that the screen was one of the most beautiful examples of needlework that they had ever seen, and I also received a letter from Her Majesty, the late Queen Mary, a patron of the Association, and a great connoisseur of *objets d'art*, who wrote, through her secretary, expressing her admiration for the beauty of the screen. The repairs cost some £130 and were so exquisitely carried out as to be undetectable. The screen is in my sitting room at Mavins End, a constant delight to my eye.

Many years ago my friend Naoroji acquired for me a valuable chest from Kathiewar. Such chests are no longer obtainable. Mine is perhaps 200 years old, and almost certainly belonged to a Maharajah, since it was the custom at the marriage of a member of the Royal Family to fill one of these chests with silks and other valuables, as a gift to the bride.

What finery must have been contained in such a chest! Mine is enormous, weighing more than three-quarters of a ton. It is made of teak, iron bound, and very elaborately decorated with brass – a splendid piece of workmanship.

Among other interesting reminders of India are three enormous vessels used for storing grain in the monsoon. They are made of heavy brass, and fitted with rings for slinging them up to the ceiling as a safeguard against rats. These vessels are about two feet in diameter and three feet high, and I imagine that they came from the establishment of a Maharajah or other such man, since they are very ornate and costly affairs for such a utilitarian purpose.

I must mention another treasure which I found, not in India, but quite by chance in Aldershot, in an antique shop. It is a large brass affair, in shape not unlike a christening font, standing about three feet high, and I was very struck with its beauty and intrigued by the coats-of-arms and other devices embossed upon it. What they represented I did not know, but I felt certain that here was something of interest.

Only this year I made a copy of the coats-of-arms and sent it to the College of Arms for elucidation. A search was made, and I received a letter from Rouge Dragon Pursuivant of Arms (I cannot refrain from mentioning this wonderful title which seems to bring colour to a humdrum world!) telling me that these arms were very interesting indeed, being those of His Royal Highness the Grand Duke of Mecklenberg, and his Consort; the Arms being surmounted by the Grand Ducal Crown, and placed upon the usual mounting lined with ermine.

The date: possibly they represented the marriage of the late Prince Henry, Duke of Mecklenberg, to Wilhelmina, Queen of the Netherlands, in 1901, or, Rouge Dragon stated, they could quite possibly be much earlier.

The use to which the article was originally put is uncertain, but the probable alternatives are rather amusing, either a christening font or a champagne cooler! I might add that I have used it as neither; it contains flowers or plants from my garden and makes a beautiful vessel for display.

Ours was a happy life and a prosperous one. In Bombay problems always awaited me on my arrival but I loved to handle them, and everything seemed to go well. We had by now installed a photogravure plant – the first used in India – and were turning out first-class work. We used it extensively for the *Illustrated Weekly of India*, started in 1910, and which was extremely popular with both the Indian and European communities and a profitable source of income. In the *Weekly* we ran competitions of the cross-word puzzle type, sometimes awarding as much as Rs. 10,000 a week in prizes, and a sizeable staff was necessary to cope with the many thousands of entries which poured in.

The editorial features of the *Weekly* were lively and topical, and the colour pages most attractive. I was fortunate enough to secure the services of a brilliant artist, Bagdatopulos, to whom I offered £5,000 for a six-months' visit to India as a member of our staff.

Bagdatopulos certainly gave us value. He worked at enormous speed, was out painting on the very first morning of his arrival when I took him to see a big firm who wanted a picture of their works.

'When can you start?' asked the Managing Director.

'Why, *now*,' said Bagdatopulos, and he set up his easel then and there, and finished his painting the same day.

After this many firms wanted to have descriptive pamphlets with illustrations carried out in colour, and Bagdatopulos produced a fine series of industrial paintings. He was a great help to us in developing our colour work, and has painted many scenes of Indian life in a manner to my mind rarely surpassed.

In due course we saw that there was a demand for an evening paper for Bombay City and the near up-country stations, and so *the Evening News of India* came into being. The daily, the weekly, and the evening papers had their own editorial and clerical staffs, and by 1930 our European employees had considerably increased, while we employed also Indians, a number of whom held executive positions. These developments, together with a continual expansion in the printing and block-making sections of the works, demanded greatly increased plant and building extensions, and we also installed an air-conditioning plant. Thereafter the office was so cool that instead of rushing away at five o'clock to change their sweaty clothes and get a drink, our men often stayed on voluntarily till 6.30 p.m., sometimes joined by their wives who appreciated relaxing in an atmosphere of under 70 degrees.

All these developments were financed out of revenue. Gone were the days when I needed to make those daring loans from the Bank. Since our staff had grown beyond anything ever visualised, it occurred to me and my fellow directors that some of the senior members who were responsible for so much of the progress made should be offered shares in the company at nominal rates. Accordingly, some 20 men were taken in as partners, and that number was gradually increased.

This was a most successful move, for now that the heads of departments felt that they had a personal stake in the business their interest was proportionately greater, and progress was made in all directions.

To stimulate this activity I held a meeting of the heads of staff in my office every Monday morning, the main item on the Agenda being: how to turn out more work, better work and faster work.

At the first meeting I took the chair. As I had anticipated; everyone listened to me most respectfully and allowed me to do all the talking. But this was not to continue. At the close of the meeting I announced that a new chairman would be appointed every week, and that I would be present to consider and discuss any suggestions put forward. I then turned to a very junior partner indeed and said, '*You* will act as Chairman at the next meeting.'

The effect was electrical. The chairman-to-be looked terrified, but also decidedly flattered and very anxious to acquit himself well, and as nobody knew until the close of any meeting who the next chairman was to be, reams of notes were made and suggestions proliferated. Some were impractical, but

I made a point of discouraging nobody. We discussed every suggestion, wild or wise, and as a result some excellent ideas emerged which were incorporated into our works practice.

Among other successful projects was the *Times of India* Book Club, which first brought me into contact with the Directors of Odhams Press. It was a book-a-month subscription scheme, the book being chosen by Odhams and handsomely produced by them. So great was the demand that our order soon rose to 30,000 copies a month. This scheme and also the competitions in the *Weekly* perforce came to an end with the beginning of World War II.

In business I was essentially a practical man, but as the years went by I had come to formulate a business philosophy, one indeed that had a wider application, for the ideas that I had applied to the conduct of work could with equal force be related to the general conduct of life.

For the benefit of our own staff I put these ideas on paper and they were printed in pamphlet form. Then friends of mine whose businesses were outside that of newspaper production asked me to issue the pamphlet to the public. I amended it and the little pamphlet had a relatively wide circulation. It contained, I believe, much sound psychology. I said that a man should learn to know himself, for 'the secret of life worth living is finding out our talents and using them to the fullest extent; finding our weaknesses and turning them into strong points.' A man should be confident, but optimism must be balanced with keen judgment and common sense. I have learnt in a small degree, that success in any business undertaking comes from thinking and seeing success instead of the possibility of failure; of trying to see good in all ideas. No V.C. has ever been won without courage and confidence in ability to succeed in the undertaking contemplated. I firmly believe that a foolish optimist is to be preferred to a clever pessimist, and I believed profoundly in the natural creativity in man, 'the desire to do.'

I believe that our business activities generally should be based as far as possible, on Christian principles, that is on the basis of good desire whereby we learn to do good for the good there is in good doing, forgetting personal gain. Have I found it easy? No! I have not always succeeded, but when I have, the results have sometimes been rather wonderful. In my private life I have learnt to treat others as I would have them treat me, to show friendship and sympathy as far as possible to others. I might give one instance illustrating this point.

One day as I was leaving my office I had a visit from a well-known motor car dealer who said he had come to ask me a special favour. I assured him that if I could help him I would do so willingly. That evening I was able to do just what he asked. It meant little to me and much to him. Early next morning he telephoned me thanking me profusely. He said he had a strong desire to show his appreciation by doing something for me in return, and had instructed his staff to cancel his advertisements in other papers and increase his advertisement space in the *Times of India*. In addition he had told them that in future all his printing orders were to be given to my firm without question of price. A short time after he again telephoned saying that he had heard that I was considering the purchase of a new car.

'You must have one of mine, and I am willing to let you have it at my cost price, which would give you a discount of 27 per cent.'

This I refused, but eventually agreed to take one of his cars at a discount of 10 per cent. The car was duly delivered and gave me much satisfaction. A friend of mine to whom I recommended the car also purchased one from this man. This was followed by a second sale to another friend. This is an example of how one good deed in business merits a generous return.

In 1938 the *Times of India* had been in existence for 100 years, and this event in the history of our newspaper was celebrated by a Centenary Dinner which took place on 14th June at Grosvenor House in London.

It was a great occasion at which I presided. Our guests, of whom there were some 300, included Lord Willingdon, at one time Viceroy of India, Lord Lamington and Sir Frederick Sykes, both retired Governors of Bombay, the Marquess of Lothian, Sir Cowasji Jehangir, Sir Hugh Stephenson, Sir John Maffey and many other men who had made their mark in India in various capacities.

Lord Willingdon said that during the war the assistance rendered by the *Times of India* was unforgettable; it had led and guided public opinion in those vital and critical years and done a great service to India and the British Empire as a whole. In my speech I recalled how one hundred years ago the *Times of India* had been issued by a handful of local traders with a capital of only a few hundred pounds, and I briefly traced the subsequent history and development of our paper. I also provided a little light relief, I hope, for I recalled how Disraeli on one occasion said that he had been reading some of the Indian daily papers and had never read anything so funny since the Arabian Nights Entertainment. He probably meant the advertisements, I said, for some were indeed very funny. There was, for instance, an advertisement inserted by a Mr Townsend, who announced the fact that he was a very experienced builder of tombs, went on to describe the excellence of the tombs which he had constructed, and ended up by saying that he trusted to receive the encouragement and patronage of all the members of St. Andrew's Church!

Sir Stanley Reed, responded to the toast of the newspaper press in India. Pressmen present represented the whole of the Empire and America, and before this notable gathering we heard the *Times of India* referred to as 'the greatest paper in Asia'.

We felt very proud of the *Times of India*, proud of our association with it, on that day.

CHAPTER 13

After we had acquired Mavins End my wife and I continued to travel to some extent, until the gradual breakdown of her health made it no longer possible. Then it was one of her great solaces to talk over some of the journeys that we had made together in the past. It helped her, I think, to forget a little the pain that increased so inexorably and resulted in her passing over in October, 1951. We had shared over 50 years of happy marriage. What the end of such a partnership means to the survivor only those who have experienced it can understand. It cannot be adequately expressed in words, nor will I try to do so.

There was a wonderful experience that we had aboard a ship steaming into Copenhagen. We were within a couple of miles of that city when the Captain and several officers rushed down from the bridge to call our attention to a strange and beautiful sight. The sky was clear and blue, except for a large white cloud, and on this cloud was reflected the city we were approaching. All the large buildings of Copenhagen could be easily distinguished on the cloud, though upside down. This 'mirage' lasted for some 15 minutes. The Captain said that in all his 35 years' at sea he had never seen or heard of such a phenomenon.

Heat, fierce blistering heat. There was an unforgettable journey that we made through the Red Sea one year in May, when the cabins were so oven-like that sleep was out of the question, and every passenger – man, woman and child – slept or tried to sleep on deck. One day we had a following wind from the desert and the heat became so unbearable that the captain actually ordered the ship to be turned around for a period in order to give the passengers a little relief. This was against all rules, and whether it was entered in his log I do not know.

We had visited Niagara. It was a wonderful experience to see the Falls as we did, from the decks of a small steamer which approached as close as safety permitted. This was on the Canadian side, where the falls are some three times wider than the American falls – about 3,000 feet, and the volume of water terrific. There was a tremendous roar, spray rose like a continuous cloud. On the Canadian side too we stood on a little platform formed by a cave situated right under the Falls, and it was an extraordinary sensation to see this mighty force of water plunge over us, completely covering the mouth of the cave, while we stood only a few feet away from it in complete safety.

At Niagara we saw what I consider to be one of the wonders of the world, a so-called 'magical' well. This well was also on the Canadian side of the Falls. It was perhaps 30 feet in diameter, and the man in charge informed us that at a depth of about 20 feet it held about 4 feet of water. He then proceeded to drop a long pipe into the water – an ordinary one-inch water pipe at the top end of which a tap was fixed.

When the man opened the tap, air rushed out with great force. He struck a match and applied it, and a flame some 5 feet long shot forth – this to our great surprise, for the pipe was not fixed but just dropped loosely into the water. Then came the greatest surprise of all. The man put both his hands into the flame, literally took out a couple of handfuls, and gave them to me! I instinctively jumped back, but on being assured that this fire did not burn, I put my handkerchief into the flame and then my hands. It was flame all right, but it had absolutely, no heat.

We were so intrigued by this well that when we returned to England I wrote to the Mayor of the place asking for an explanation. He replied that there was none; no scientist had ever explained this phenomenon. All he could tell me was that a hundred or more years before the well had been worshipped as a God of great power by the Red Indians – and apparently the power still remained.

On one occasion we saw a water spout, not an uncommon sight, but an alarming one, if it happens to be at sea. We had occasionally seen water spouts from the high hills round Bombay, but on this occasion we were sailing up the Adriatic when we almost ran into one of these cloudbursts. The Captain had to alter course completely to avoid it, and he told me later that if this waterspout had fallen on the ship, we should certainly have sunk.

Sometimes a severe cloudburst sheds water with such force that when it reaches the sea it throws up waves ten feet high. We remembered seeing one at a place on the north coast of Italy, and first noticed it a mile out at sea. In an incredibly short space of time it seemed to cross a small bay near where we were standing and travel inland and then there was a roaring sound. After its passing, we found that the road where it had struck had been torn up as if by an avalanche. When such severe cloudbursts occur, the water seems to come down in a confined space as a solid mass, like ten thousand taps being turned on simultaneously! It is, of course, much more concentrated than rainfall, though I remember one year in Bombay when 23 inches fell in one day – the equivalent of a whole year's rain in London! Comparing rainfalls, in Bombay City the average is some 80 inches in the three monsoon months; outside on the hills at places like Mahableshwar, it is some 250 to 300 inches for the same period. A place to avoid must be Cherrapunji in Assam, where the annual average is 600 inches – the heaviest rainfall in the world.

This brief record of my impressions is drawing to a close, for soon, with the sale of the *Times of India* I was to say farewell to Bombay and the greater part of my life's work, and it is here that I choose to close my book. It is an artificial ending, of course, for now, a decade later, my life goes on, new interests unfold, and the energy that I still retain I have transferred to other fields.

I have, for example, come to love South Africa and now, when the fogs begin to descend on England and winter approaches, I make for Capetown, just as in former days my target was Bombay. I have friends in South Africa, I have business interests there, I travel, and I love it very much.

I have visited the Victoria Falls in Central Africa discovered by Dr Livingstone just over a hundred years ago, and still far less known than Niagara. They are a tremendous sight. They are formed by the River Zambesi plunging over a series of cliffs some four hundred feet high and a mile wide, and falling in an irregular zig-zag formation. I cannot convey the impression the Falls give of power and immensity and of delicacy too. As much as twenty miles away one can see huge columns of spray rising up from the chasm - a tremendous column of smoke-like vapour hanging forever above the huge tumbling masses of water.

My friends and I donned mackintoshes and walked through the Rain Forest, which runs for a short distance along the edge of the chasm opposite to the Falls. Owing to the continuous clouds of spray from the Falls this forest is soaked in moisture throughout the year and hence its name. It is full of unusual trees, tropical palms, wild flowers and maidenhair ferns, and it is a very lovely sight. But most wonderful of all were the rainbows – imagine 13 arcs in the sky all at once, which is what we saw. One rainbow was a triple, several were double, the rest single.

I was fortunate to visit the Falls at full moon, when we saw what is known as a lunar rainbow – something I had never heard of. A midnight rainbow without colour, a pale white opalescent mystic aura, stretched from the waters four hundred feet below to a point some three hundred feet above the roaring falls. This spectral rainbow, the endless clouds of fine spray glinting in the moonlight, and the tumult of the waters, made an unforgettable scene.

My interest in wild life naturally took me to Kruger Park, South Africa's great Game Reserve – not a park in our sense of the word, but an enormous area of some 8,000 square miles of primitive bush, forest and plain, with the great Drakensburg Mountains running along the western edge. There are no villages in the Reserve, which is given over exclusively to animals. Thousands of miles of roads intersect the Reserve, travel by car only is permitted, and visitors may not leave their cars except at the rest camps provided. An additional precaution is that they must be in camp before sundown and may not leave before sunrise. The reason for these safety measures soon becomes apparent, for lions and other wild animals roam freely, often within a few feet of one's car.

I spent three days in the Reserve, travelling some 250 miles in the Southern sector. Those few days were full of thrills. We encountered our first when we saw some six yards off the road two female lions on a kill. To see a lion in its natural surroundings, free and uncontrolled, while sitting in a car only a few feet away, is an extraordinary sensation. On this occasion as our driver pulled up, he calmly lit a cigarette and sat smoking as peacefully as though at his own fireside! Meanwhile the lions, quite oblivious of their audience, continued their feast until one, having had her fill, got up and walked away to sleep in the shelter of a small bush. The other lioness dragged the remainder of the Impala she was devouring out of the sun and continued her meal in the shade.

Later that day we came on another pair – a lioness and a magnificent specimen of a blackmaned lion. He was sitting only a yard off the road in a position typical of Landseer's lions in Trafalgar Square; a superb creature, a perfect specimen of fitness and strength, dignified, regal. But the monarch was quite unconcerned with our car and its occupants. His only preoccupation for the moment seemed to be his sleeping wife, who was lying on her back quite close with her paws in the air. We left this pair, but returning an hour later, found the lioness in precisely the same position, still slumbering. The male had however, evidently been disturbed, for he was moving around and showing signs of lameness. He may have fought with another Blackmane known to be in the neighbourhood, and gave an occasional growl, more due to his injury than to resentment of us, for he completely ignored our car.

In our journey through the Reserve we encountered herds of wildebeest – big ox-like animals – dozens of kooloo and impala, which are attractive little antelopes, water buck, the smaller stein buck and duiler. We saw in addition a number of zebra, half a dozen hippopotami sleeping away the hours in the river, troops of baboon, some of whom were rather ferocious looking monsters, a number of blue monkeys, a dozen or so warthogs, and a solitary jackal. The most impressive sight was, perhaps, an enormous giraffe, some twenty feet high, which seemed to sail along, passing within a few yards of our car, forever on the lookout for Master Lion, for the giraffe provides the lion with meat for many days. There are many leopards in the Reserve, but they feed on smaller game. In numbers we must, I think, have seen some thousand animals in our trek, a satisfactory return for a longish journey by rail and car.

An interesting spectacle which I saw in Durban one year was the annual N'Goma Dancing Competition between teams of Zulus, most of them employees of the local business firms. There is tremendous enthusiasm for this competition and the performers practise assiduously for months before the opening contest.

Each team has from 40 to 80 men, whose dress consists of nodding head decorations of turkey feathers, the characteristic calf-skin skirts hanging in the rear from the waist, and anklets of seeds which rattle with the movement of the feet and add to the precision effect of the performance. The dancers are armed with sticks decorated with leopard skin bindings, representing the spear of the ancient Zulu, shields of buckskin, the whole representing as nearly as possible the dress and arms of the original 'orthodox' Zulu Impis.

The competition finals attract a huge crowd of some 10,000 people and the exhibition is extraordinarily attractive. It is difficult to describe the actual dance. It seems to be made up of a variety of foot movements, body turnings and bendings in which the manipulation of the shields and spears play a prominent part. The stamping of the feet is accompanied by guttural shouts emitted with astonishing rhythm. It is a wild, fascinating barbaric show, performed with perfect control and in perfect tempo, The band, an important adjunct, consists of

40 or more performers with pairs of wooden clappers or battens which they strike together, so timing all the movements of the dancers.

But let the rattle and stamping of the dancers fade as I switch my mind back to India, and to the astonishing incident which led to the end of my life's work in Bombay.

In spite of political developments we had never contemplated selling the *Times of India*, but in a sense, our hand was forced. It is a strange story and I give it in some detail.

One day I received a call from a certain Mr Dalmia, who was then staying at the Taj Mahal Hotel in Bombay. He intimated that he would like to see me on a private matter and as he did not wish to discuss this in my office he asked me if I would meet him at the hotel.

I agreed, we met, and this extraordinary man announced immediately, 'Mr Pearson, I am going to buy the *Times of India* and all your other papers.'

Dumfounded, I said to him, 'You are not going to buy them – the business is not for sale!'

'Oh, yes, Mr Pearson, I am buying it!' said Dalmia, and he proceeded to tell me that although he had never set foot in the office or works, had no knowledge of the profits, seen none of the books or balance sheets and did not ask to see them, he was quite fixed in his intentions.

'I am not at all concerned with profits,' said Dalmia. 'I want the papers for the influence they command, and I am quite prepared to pay almost any price to get them.'

Mr Dalmia proceeded to explain that when the new Government came into force it was rumoured that they would decide that in the case of British owned concerns in the country, 75 per cent of the shares would be held by Indians and only the remaining 25 per cent be retained by Europeans, and that shares would have to be transferred at nominal prices. He added that he was informed that some 30 or more of our senior employees, both Indian and European, had in the past few years been allotted a proportion of our shares at nominal prices, and remarked shrewdly, 'If I make you and all your shareholders an offer of six times the nominal value of the shares, how can the small employee shareholders refuse such an offer?'

'Because I shall ask them not to sell at any price,' I said.

Our interview then closed, but in due course Mr Dalmia wrote to me confirming his verbal offer. He stipulated, however, that he would buy only on condition that he acquired the whole of the shares issued so that he could assume complete control.

I immediately called a meeting of the employee shareholders and put the whole matter before them. I hoped against hope that they would refuse to sell, but some seemed to think the offer too good to turn down, and indeed, to a small holder of say, £1,000 or £1,500 to receive six times that amount was more than tempting for it represented a fortune.

'Think it over carefully,' I said to the men, 'and come and see me tomorrow with your agreed decision.'

Next day they came. All had decided in favour of selling.

Dalmia had promised me that if we agreed to sell he would give me a cheque for the equivalent of a million pounds forthwith on account. On learning of our decision, he promptly sent me a cheque for about one and three quarter million pounds; and in due course the transfer was made accordingly. My only condition was that none of the European employees under contract should be sent away in under three years if they wished to remain on the staff. A very few decided to stay on, but now no member of the original staff remains on the paper.

The sale of the *Times of India* took place in 1946, exactly ten years ago. Parting with the paper was a great wrench to me, not unlike that of a parent parting with its child, for I had put so much of my life into it. Now I had to adjust to a new pattern.

Today my life is once again absorbing. I have many friends, and my interests in England and in South Africa keep me occupied and alert. I have known so much happiness and fulfilment that I do not lament the years that are ended. Rather,

I re-live them in memory as I have done in these pages, and as the past mingles with the present both bring their own particular joy, and I am content.

Editor's Postscript

My own recollections of Ted are clear. As my grandfather Harry, an Aldershot farmer, and Ciss, his sister, were very close, on Harry's death aged 38, Ciss and Ted became heavily involved with our family.

For reasons of trying to redress an imbalance in an inheritance, Ted offered to pay my brother's school fees and Edie my grandmother paid for mine. I was of average intelligence, but diligent. My brother Ian clung happily onto the lowest rung of the 'Could do better' category. There was, therefore, the thrice yearly nightmare of having to show Ian's school report to Uncle Ted.

Ciss always tried to diffuse the situation by sending us out into the garden below her balcony and, calling 'It's snowing', would sprinkle 10 shilling notes on us!

None of Ian's reports were good and eventually he was put onto a weekly report, which involved getting a comment from every teacher, after every lesson. This was to be shown to the headmaster every week.

The two reports of which he was most proud were the master of Greek writing in large letters 'DIM', and another who wrote 'This boy has the makings of an oaf!'. Fortunately Ted was not privy to these.

Ian subsequently had a very successful career and has made a great success of his life. He is now living in the Yorkshire Dales and causing only minor havoc.

Ted died in 1958, the house was sold to the widow of a film magnate who was downsizing and looking for a 'country cottage'. The contents alone raised over £4,000 pounds.

BERT

HERBERT CECIL PATRICK

Bert's love letter from Amy

Bert, far right, at the British School on steps
from Farnham Castle.

From the notes and recollections of Sally Gaudern, his granddaughter

Herbert Patrick was born in Farnham, Surrey, in 1882. His mother was Alice Patrick, née Croucher, wife of Henry Ratcliffe Patrick. Herbert was the eldest of her five children, there being four sons and one daughter.

Herbert attended the British School in East Street, Farnham. The only documentation I have from his childhood are several love letters dated 1891 from his sweetheart, Amy, aged 9 years old, who lived at 209 New Cross Road, London.

In 1899, when he was 17 years old, Herbert joined the Queen's Regiment Volunteers. Two years later the 1901 census finds him in Bury St Edmunds residing as a lodger with Sarah Ann Carter. Her home is at 4 Cemetery Road and Herbert is working as an apprentice Monumental Letter Cutter.

The 1900 Trade Directory lists two firms to which he may have been apprenticed, both in Cemetery Road: Frederick Herbert Goddard or Arthur Henry Hanchet (at number 158).

At the time of the South African War, Herbert was serving in the Volunteer Company of the Queen's Royal West Surrey Regiment and was keen to go out to South Africa. He was too young to join the first service company in 1901, but he was included in the second service company in 1902 when peace was declared.

Herbert volunteered for the South African Mounted Constabulary but failed the medical examination because although perfectly fit, he had a slight predisposition to varicose veins. A month later he applied to join the Chartered Company's Mounted Police in Rhodesia.

He was anxious when he found his medical examination was to be conducted by the same doctor who had recently failed him. Fortunately he was not recognised and he was passed fit for service. His card was marked 'Slight tendency to varicose veins, but not likely to prove detrimental to his work.'

Bert paid his own passage to Cape Town, and found that the Mounted Police were the defence force of the country. After military training, including mounted exercises and mounted musketry, he was posted to his first outstation at Gwanda. He attested in the B.S.A.P. [British South Africa Police] on 28th July 1905.

B.S.A. POLICE, SOUTHERN RHODESIA

Gwanda Police Camp

After the Matabele rebellion it was decided to amalgamate the police provinces, instead of having separate Mashonaland and Matabeleland commands. This resulted in the troops being rearranged as follows:

A Troop was established with headquarters in Salisbury
B Troop at Goromonzi
C Troop at Sinoia
D Troop at Umatali
E Troop at Salisbury depot
F Troop at Fort Victoria
G Troop at Gwanda
H Troop at Gwelo
J Troop at Filabusi
K Troop at Bulawayo
L Troop at Fort Usher

The first mention of Gwanda police station, the home of A Troop, is in the year 1896 when the Matabeleland and

Mashonaland divisions were merged together and the troop letters were changed.

At that time the Post was established at the south bank of the Manzimayama River about three-quarters of a mile south east of the present site on the main road to West Nicholson. It was decided that this was a highly dangerous locality from a military point of view, as the camp was wide open to attack. So in 1902 or 1903 it was moved to the site it is on today. The hill directly behind the camp was duly prepared for occupation in the event of an uprising. The larger stations were known as Forts.

Fort Filabusi was in the form of a pole and dagga stockade. Eight foot high, and enclosing an area 30 yards by 18 yards, with a surrounding trench 8 feet wide by 6 feet deep, its excavated earth was thrown up against the walls of the stockade.

The outstations were of the same pattern if slightly smaller. Inside each fort were somehow crowded two pole and dagga buildings, with doors and window frames knocked up from discarded packing cases, used as a ration store and a guard room. Again somehow crowded into the confined space of the fort, a raised walkway of compacted earth ran round the inside of the stockade, to enable sentries to peep over the top. Full guard duties in these forts were soon discontinued as none of the forts were subjected to attack.

In approximately 1900 Tuli surrendered its Magistracy to Gwanda, as it was then, and it became an official Government Post.

To give an idea what Gwanda was like at this time, here is a line from the diary of Captain H.P. Tuckey, 5th New Zealand Regiment, dated 18th July 1900, writing home from the Manzimayama Hotel on route to Tuli. 'The place consists of a store and hotel combined and a police camp with a dozen huts.'

The Police camp at this time consisted of wooden and iron buildings. The staff included a captain, a sergeant-in-charge, three or four corporals, a saddler corporal and about 15 troopers, excluding the African Police. There was also a farrier.

In the early 1900s after the outbreak of horse sickness in Southern Rhodesia the Police sought an alternative to the horse as a method of transport for patrolling the country districts.

Colonel J.T.E. Flint of the Police who had served in the Army in India was instructed to proceed to India and procure camels as a replacement for the horse in certain areas of the country. Camel stables were then erected.

Colonel Flint returned to Rhodesia with a number of camels, although it is not known exactly how many. The camels were accompanied by Sikh camel drivers to supply the knowledge needed for their care and handling. It is known that these camels were employed at Goromonzi in Mashonaland, and Gwanda in Matabeleland. The camels were used over a number of years, but were not a success as the type of terrain traversed was much too hard for their feet.

Another problem was the close proximity of horses and mules, as they are animals that are fearful of the camel. Photographs of this time always show a handler with each camel, horse and mule, firmly holding the bridles and the mules are always blindfolded as well.

Photos taken just prior to the First World War show camels bringing the mail from Fort Tuli to Gwanda. The camel stables then became the European mess. These original camel stables still stand today and house the CID Section.

The country was noted for its infinite variety of game, ranging from elephants downwards, and they shot most of their food.

Life in the Mounted Police was largely patrol work, riding out on patrol for two weeks at a stretch. The first job was always to light a fire when setting up camp for the night to keep the lions away from the horses.

The Mounted Police's job was principally to collect hut taxes from the natives, who did not see why they should pay them. Bert remarked 'I didn't see why they should either'. The tax was levied according to the number of huts a man had in his kraal.

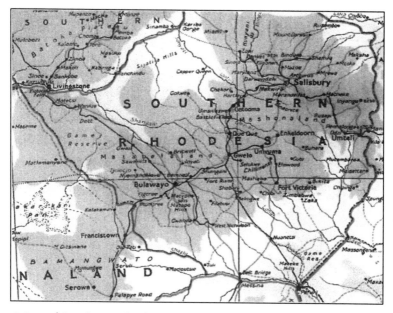

Map of Southern Rhodesia taken from old Philips World Atlas.

Bert, centre, with camels at Gwanda.

Bert with ostriches, Gwanda 1905.

British South African Police 1905. Bert back
row 4th from left.

Bert had never known finer men than the Matabele. They were fine specimens of manhood, straight as a gun barrel in their dealings and their women were strictly moral. During six weeks patrolling in the bush he had been in parts of Matabeleland where natives had never seen a white man before. He was upset at how badly the Matabele had been treated. The white man just overran the country. There were native reserves of course but they had no ownership of land.

Bert recalled: 'I was a good deal among them and I got to understand them. One old chief whose name was "Dopey" had been a chief of staff during the rebellion, took a fancy to me, and I was always welcome at his kraal. He invariably provided chicken to entertain me and made a great fuss of me. As I have said the women were absolutely moral but on one occasion Dopey offered me his daughter in marriage. This is the greatest compliment a Matabele can pay you, to offer you one of their women. The chief gave me the name Massa Tabula, meaning "the quiet one" as I was always quiet when talking to his natives.'

Interesting events occurred when natives working in the mines became drunk from a potent concoction of beer distilled from mealies. Then ructions started and the police would be called. Bert bore a scar on his right arm for life as the result of a wound inflicted by an assegai sword.

In another incident a man was arrested in connection with the theft of some gold, and after he had broken out of goal three times, he was then taken to the stone goal at Gwanda. Bert sat all night with his back to the cell door. Later the prisoner escaped again before his trial, but was again captured. He had wandered for 200 miles in the bush, and his nerve had gone.

There was more trouble when Bert had to deal with a hold up of a coach carrying gold from the mines. 'The search lasted months. Eventually the gold was found but not the man responsible for the hold up, until one of my troop, talking loudly, gave the game away. It was one of our own men. It was alleged he was wanted for murder before he joined the police but this was never proved. He was an Irishman and got a stiff sentence.

'Four out of six men in the force were either public school men, remittance men, misfits from the Army, Navy or the Church but they were some of the finest men you could wish to live with. I was there for over two years and then went down with Dengue Fever for six months. I was offered three months' sick leave in Cape Town but preferred to take my discharge.'

Bert was discharged 'By Purchase' on 3rd August 1907. The nominal roll states he was discharged with the rank of trooper, but his discharge certificate states he held the rank of 'Staff Corporal'. Photographs show he is wearing corporal's stripes. It has been suggested with his background in the building industry, he would be acting in a pioneer roll to have this rank at Gwanda.

HOME FROM RHODESIA

Bert sailed home from Cape Town, on 'R.M.S. Kenilworth Castle' on 7th August 1907, which was under the command of Captain J. Morton. 'Kenilworth Castle' had been built by Messrs Harland and Wolff of Belfast. Its tonnage was 12,975 tons, length 570 feet, breadth 64 feet and depth 38 feet.

The entertainments programme on board ship included: 'Athletic Sports, Thursday and Friday, August 15th and 16th, commencing each day at 2 p.m. Fancy Dress Ball Friday 16th August at 8.30 p.m.'

More Athletic Sports were scheduled at 10 a.m. on the same days, maybe for different sections of passengers as the results are divided into Tournaments 1st, 2nd and 3rd class. Also the sports results are in class order. Tournaments are divided into: rubber quoits, rope quoits and bucket quoits.

REASON FOR RETURNING FROM RHODESIA

Bert's mother Alice had died in October 1903, two weeks after giving birth to Alice Violet, her only daughter, who had been born on 16th October 1903. Bert's father Henry, although a very loveable man, had no head for business. The family firm was in poor shape after the emigration of his two eldest sons, Bert and Ernest, and the death of his wife.

Henry had been left with Sydney and Harold, his younger two sons after the death of Alice. The age gap between Bert, the eldest, and Violet, the youngest, was nearly 21 years, and Harold was only two years old when Violet was born.

Violet had been taken in by Nurse Phillips, the local midwife, when Alice died, and was brought up by her. Violet was profoundly deaf all her life and as life was not easy for her, Nurse Phillips arranged for Violet to be married to a train driver named Albert Smith, so she would be well cared for after Nurse Phillips' death.

On returning from Rhodesia in 1907 Bert took over his grandfather's business premises in Union Road. Trading under his own name, H.C. Patrick, he set about reviving the family fortunes. He also found a wife, Daisy Wing, whom he married soon after his return from Africa.

In 1909 it was decided to go actively into the funeral furnishing business, which was at that time almost entirely in the hands of local builders. From then on the business's progress was rapid and a move was made into new premises in East Street.

Bert joined the Surrey Yeomanry in 1913 and the business was left in the hands of Bert's brother, Sydney Patrick. He too joined up in 1917, and the business was run by W. Bloxham, foreman, and Daisy, his wife.

A sad and all too frequent duty was to make the whole day journey with pony and trap, in times of an epidemic of diphtheria, smallpox, or scarlet fever, to visit an Isolation Hospital beyond Guildford to bring back the bodies of the small children who had died.

Bert and Daisy had five children, Eric, Eileen, Joyce, Norman and Lorna, born between 1908 and 1915.

MILITARY CAREER

1913 Surrey Yeomanry

On 13th February 1913 Bert enlisted into the Surrey Yeomanry, Queen Mary's Regiment. He was accepted for service and was made Private 1658.

Bert's regiment was a mounted unit of the Territorial Force (TF) and had been formed when the TF came into being on 1st April 1908. It was headquartered in Melbourne House in Clapham Park but Bert was probably enlisted into B Squadron, which was at Guildford, with drill stations at Woking and Camberley.

The legal terms under which Bert joined the army were specific to the units of the TF. Before the war this was a part-time form of soldiering. The man enlisted for four years' service, with the condition that he reported for a number of drills and that he attend the two-week summer camps. Under the terms he was not obliged to serve overseas. Those men who were already serving received a mobilisation notice and were 'embodied' for full time service on 5th August 1914.

In 1914 Sergeant H.C. Patrick was sent home from front line, seriously ill with appendicitis to a Camberwell hospital.

Bert recovered and embarked for service in France on 16th January 1915. He was certainly with B Squadron at this time.

Soon after mobilisation the regiment concentrated and moved to Kent. It was then split up, each Squadron being placed under orders of a different infantry Division, to act as a mobile arm of that Division. B Squadron moved to Winchester where it came under the orders of 28th Division on 22nd December 1914.

By this date, all men had been asked to sign the 'Imperial Service Obligation', an additional agreement that allowed the army to use them overseas. Those men who did not wish to sign were removed to form a reserve unit (this became known as the 2/1st Surrey Yeomanry, while the original became 1/1st). Their places were taken by new recruits who had signed on enlisting.

B Squadron landed at Le Havre on 18th January 1915, and served in Flanders for most of the rest of the year. The Squadron sailed for Salonika from Marseilles on 4th November 1915, where they stayed for the rest of the war. Bert however was discharged from the ranks the day before he was commissioned into the Army Ordnance Corps i.e. 28th August 1915 having reached the rank of Sergeant. He was commissioned on 29th August 1915.

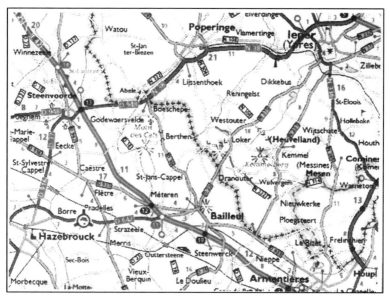

Map of area where Surrey Yeomanry were stationed 1914.
Bert was here until Commissioned in1915.

Summary of the movements of B Squadron in France from February to August 1915

1st February 1915

In billets at Pradelles (just east of Hazebrouck in Nord, France) having moved there from Le Havre. Many men ill with colds and sore throats.

2nd February

Moved to camp one mile outside Poperinge, going via Fletre, Meteren, Bailleul, Locre and Zevekoten.

8th February

Had to provide a detachment to act as Mounted Police.

10th February

One Troop ordered to search area in rear of trenches for presence of enemy snipers. (Location likely to be in the Wulvergem-Wijtschate area.) This duty continued, one Troops taking over each 24 hours until 19th February.

19th February

Routine duties in camp until 28th February.

1st March

Remained at camp, 'not actively employed' until 28th March.

28th March

Marched to C Camp, Vlamertinghe, which comprised canvas sided huts. Continued at same location until 10th April.

10th April

Moved to 'disgustingly filthy' billets near the aerodrome, Poperinghe. (No aerodromes are shown in later maps near Poperinghe.) One officer and 30 men were detached for duty with V Corps.

23rd April

Ordered to stand by.

(Late on 22nd April, the Germans had launched an attack north east of Ypres, employing poison chlorine gas for the first time in history. The gas rolled across two Divisions of French troops, holding the front at that sector. Not unnaturally, the defenceless troops broke and for some hours there was a large gap in the line. It was filled most gallantly during the evening and night by the Canadian Division, who held off a further German advance. Both sides quickly moved reserves into the area and the conflict grew into a major battle now known as the Second Battle of Ypres. 28th Division was heavily engaged. But even in this, the troops of B Squadron were not called upon.)

27th April

Moved into billets at a farm north-east of Vlamertinghe and about one mile from that place. Routine continued. (This may be the location later known as Cat Farm. It no longer exists, being under the modern Ypres by-pass road.)

14th May

Moved to Hoendebrugge. (This may be Haende-Brugge, a hamlet between Winnezeele and Steenvoorde.)

17th May

Marched back to Vlamertinghe. The squadron was attached to 3rd Cavalry Division for fatigue duties, but was only used once for filling sandbags.

21st May

Returned to orders of 28th Division and returned to old billets of Vlamertinghe.

25th-26th May

For 36 hours squadron provided standing patrols on roads west of Ypres.

30th May

Marched to Watou. (Watou is west of Poperinghe.)

14th June

Marched to billets one mile south-west of Reninghelst. Provided 10 men for Military Police.

24th June

Marched to billets one mile east of Westoutre. Provided a guard of one NCO and four men for water supply at Dickebusch. (Now called Dikkebus, south-west of Ypres.)

20th July

Marched to Strazeele. Spent a week destroying sandbags which had been affected by fire.

28th July

Marched back to Westoutre. Trench digging parties at night. It was impossible to send parties of 50 men, and a change to 30 was introduced.

August 1915

The trenches being dug are described as a 'subsidiary' or 'switch' line. This is a reserve defensive position, along which men can be easily and relatively safely moved from one area to another. The position 9th – 13th August is noted as being near Dismal Villa, and from 13th –31st August at the Sherpenberg. (The name Dismal Villa is not marked on British maps and appears to have fallen into disuse by the end of 1915. The Scherpenberg is a hill, the summit of which is shown on the above map, south-west of Loker.)

During this month great difficulty was experienced with the horses, on account of shortage of men. 'Horses got fatter but rapidly lost working condition'.

There are no military records of Bert's service in the Army Ordnance Corps before 1918, although he was known to be a munitions expert. He appears as a signatory as DADOS i.e. Deputy Assistant Director of Ordnance services to 40th Division in January 1919. This office was based at Roubaix, north-east of Lille.

He was also possibly ADOS (Assistant Director of Ordnance Services) to XV Corps. It is thought he was there in a staff role but was not senior enough to be a signatory.

A Division comprised of about 20,000 men, a Corps commanded two or three Divisions.

On returning from the war Bert brought his horse home from France.

July 13ᵗʰ
1919

Dear Dada

I am writing you your last letter while you are in the army. I have got such a ripping suit Mum has bought me and it cost £3 – 3s but as mum said, it is good cloth and fits me exactly. I was top in Exams first in Arithmetic, Drawing, Spelling, and I have not yet heard the report of the Writing which we shall hear of on Monday, I have been top in everything so far, and I expect I shall be top in Writing. We went to our sports picnic out to the Devils Jumps Thursday and we had hide and seek, tip it and run, rounders races, scrambles for sweets and all sorts of games among which were egg cap, and I won a jolly fine purse in the races and we had a fine time. Then on Friday we had a cricket match all the afternoon. I and Blake picked won the first toss and had first

Eric's letter to Bert, 1ˢᵗ page

2

pick. But Blake is far the strongest boy
in the school and biggest and oldest too,
but he ~~slog~~ slogs too much and does not
wait for his bowls to see whether they
are going to break or not ~~altogether~~ altogether
their side were too careless and did not play
half so well as they could, and we had
them all out in a quarter of an hour with
19 runs, our wicket-keeper let no byes,
whereas theirs let 19 ~~byes~~ byes. Well to
cut a long ~~story~~ short, when it ~~is~~ was
time they had 19 runs, and we had 111
(a hundred and eleven) by playing steady,
of which I hit 66, the only ~~obly o th~~
others got 26 between them and as I said
before we got 19 byes, and Miss Stroud
promised me sixpence for playing
so well for I besides my runs, ~~fiv~~
had four out when they ~~were~~ in, and the
best of all was that in my ~~fift~~
fifth over as batsmen, I got the
ball in my eye just on the brow
and by the time I got home

Eric's letter 2nd page

3

I had a black eye bigger than a walnut, but still, fortunetly my eyesight was alright, but it did not half put the wind-up old Mum at first, when I got home, but it has gone down now but it is still swollen up and is fearfully black, but still I got my sixpence next day, but as Mum says if it had been a half an inch lower it would have to knocked my eye out. Well I must say I have something to decorate me for the ... Must close now love

Eric

X X X X X X X

P.S. So glad you are coming home home for good on the 16th or about then. In the cricket match I forgot to tell you it took the other side half an hour and 25 minuts to get to get us out.

Eric's letter 3rd page

Bert, signing for stores at Roubaix. 1919.
DADOS, Deputy Assistant Director of Services, 40th Division.

POST WAR RECORD

(Details from this section taken from *Farnham in War and Peace*, W. Ewbank-Smith, Phillimore & Co Ltd, 1983.)

After the war, funeral work at Bert's firm increased substantially, and horses and rolling stock were added to the small equipment up to that time owned by the firm.

Large contracts for the Imperial War Graves Commission were carried out, and with a rapidly increasing turnover in monumental masonry, development was rapid. Modern stone-working plant and machinery were installed, and by the end of the War Graves contracts the firm was one of the best equipped in the south of England.

1920

Major Patrick's tender was accepted by the War Memorial Committee for the erection of a memorial in Gostrey Meadow. Work was commenced in December and expected to take three months.

In addition, the War Graves Commission awarded Patrick's the contract for the supply of 400 headstones for British soldiers' graves in France. Each stone was to be inscribed with the name and number, the crest of the dead man's regiment, and an emblem of his religion. Relatives were also able to add a personal inscription if they wished.

1921

The memorial cross for Gostrey went on display in Patrick's window in East Street. The council wished to discover the names of those who had died. The list so far contained 202 names – 64 in the town area, 105 in Hale and 33 in Badshot Lea. By the time the list closed, so that Patrick's firm might set about engraving the names on the panels, the number had risen to 267. That was about 13.3 per cent of the 2,000-odd men of the urban district who had served in the forces, or 2 per cent of the district's entire population.

1923

Patrick's won an order from the War Graves Commission for 681 headstones for the graves of unknown soldiers in Flanders, and in July an order for a further 2,000. The stones were to be lettered:

A SOLDIER OF THE GREAT WAR
KNOWN UNTO GOD

Visitors to First World War cemeteries might find, on closer inspection, the signature H.C.P. on many of the memorials.

1924

In May the firm secured orders for carved tablets in the cemetery in Jerusalem.

In July a contract for four 18 feet high memorials to the Indian forces who fell in Mesopotamia to be erected in Alwiyah and Baghdad inscribed in Urdu, Hindi and Gurmukhi.

They also carved inscription panels on New Zealand memorials for the Twelve Tree Copse Cemetery and the Hill 60 Cemetery both in Gallipoli.

1926

Patrick's received a contract for the name-panels on the Menin Gate memorial then being erected at Ypres – a particular honour since there were several hundred monumental masons in the field. The gate was designed by Sir Reginald Blomfield.

Patrick's also won an order from the Imperial War Graves Commission for headstones in East Africa.

1931

The latest order from the War Graves Commission won by the firm was for a Portland stone plaque commemorating the men who gave their lives at the mole at Zeebrugge on St George's Day 1918 thus blocking the harbour used by the German U-boats.

1932

Rev J. Penry-Davey, ex-Army Chaplain and a man of outstanding personality, arrived in March to take the place of Mr Layton at the Congregational Church. [Editor's note: The Rev Penry-Davey's son, Samuel Watson Penry-Davey later married Bert's youngest daughter, Lorna.]

POST WAR FAMILY MATTERS

In 1924 Bert had a lovely new house built, in Old Compton Lane, Farnham, designed by Harold Falkner. The family were delighted with their new home, having previously always lived 'over the shop'. The house had a beautiful stone facade and delightful garden, with a tennis court, an orchard and plenty of room at the back for a large chicken run. There was also a garage with a pigeon coop in the roof, and a large vegetable garden to the front of the property. He called the house GWANDA (after his posting in Southern Rhodesia).

The children attended St Mary's Church, Compton, every Sunday and went to Sunday School whilst Bert attended the Parish church of St Andrew's in the centre of Farnham. Instead of attending Church the children usually went scrumping apples or birds' nesting. On their return they were questioned on the Sermon. Unfortunately Bert's great friend Ernie Langham, proprietor of the *Farnham Herald*, also went to Compton Church and always came in for a sherry before lunch. The children's version of the week's sermon and his often conflicted which resulted in great wrath and fearsome punishments.

Editor's note: Eric, my father, when aged about 17 years, was involved in a fight over a girl when he was at a dance at the Congregational Hall. It spilled out into the street and he suffered a bloody nose. Later he rushed home to his mother, Daisy, who washed his white but bloody shirt quickly and hid it. They thought all was well. However several days later Ernie Langham said to Bert 'Poor show that, Bert, your boy brawling in the street, poor show.' Bert was home in a flash and Eric got a sound thrashing.

Rifle Shooting at Bisley Camp

Bert had a lifelong interest in rifle shooting. He captained the Surrey team for many years, and even had his own bedroom in the Surrey Hut. Daisy always remarked somewhat cynically that when she died he would be at Bisley. And so he was.

1930

A national newspaper quoted 'A notable rifle shooting record was established by Mr H.C. Patrick of Farnham at the recent Bisley meeting. He was in every prize list except one, and he entered every competition.

He made a possible in the *Times* competition, 20 out of nearly 1,000 competitors also doing so. In the shoot off he secured third place winning the bronze cross and a good cash prize. This shoot he describes as the stiffest he has ever had.

In the *Daily Telegraph* competition he scored 34 out of 35 at 600 yards which brought him near the top of the prize list, while in the St George's vase competition he was placed into the final with a score of 48 out of 50.

Bert with Daily Telegraph cup. Bisley.

Ernie Langham, Bert and Morris with Penny
Farthing found in Compton Woods.

He was 5th in the City of London corporation competition, a 1,000 yards shoot scoring 49 out of 50.

He got through the first stage of the King's Prize competition but failed to qualify for the final. On the same day he became the proud possessor of an international badge shooting in England's twenty in the international match, which was won by Scotland.

In the English Twenty Club Championship he was placed 6th winning the bronze badge.

The greatest honour of all was that he was runner up in the grand aggregate, thus winning the silver cross. He was then chosen for the international team. He shot for Surrey in the county championships, the winners being Sussex.

1950

At the AGM of The Surrey Rifle Association, Bert, along with Major Talbot Smith, were presented with silver salvers by Sir Robert Haining, President of the Surrey Rifle Association and Lord Lieutenant of Surrey, in recognition of 50 years' service at Bisley to the Surrey Teams.

The Chairman, Colonel Chetwynd-Stapylton, gave a brief summary of the shooting records of the two men.

Excerpts from Bert's Diary 1937 – 1945

My Diary from 1st August 1937.

It will be of most interest to myself in writing it. Decide to start a diary in order that I may have a record of happenings and my thoughts – which may serve for guidance in future.

1st August 1937

Very black beginning owing the death of my Mickey [his dog], but Church helped, and then worked till one o'clock in my office, kept my mind functioning as usual.

Home for half an hour then walked to Badshot Lea and back via prehistoric pit dwellings just discovered, which are extraordinary because it is impossible to see aught but simple holes in the ground. Through Park to Castle Cafe for tea, then to office for more work on Eileen's house.

5th August

Rotary today went off well, we passed a resolution to drink to Rotary the world over at the conclusion of our weekly meetings.

7th August

A busy morning working till three o'clock. Norman and Tom very busy. I get much satisfaction out of working on Saturday afternoons. I feel I have really set an example which I am always anxious to do.

Met my friend Ernie Langham at four o'clock and we had a most wonderful walk to Crondall through field paths and woods. So delightful in the still intense heat. Arrived at Crondall and had tea at the Cricketers, simple and lovely but so enjoyable. Ern and I had tea in the garden and the bread and fresh butter with most refreshing tea and home-made cakes, one of the most delightful meals I have had for a long time.

And then still to explore more mysteries on the way home. We both wanted to find Dora's Green and after rambling through brick works and more fields we found it. Every road and track from all around the compass was signposted to Dora's Green, and strangers must think it a place of great importance. It is anything but, a few modern with perhaps one or two older but thoroughly uninteresting cottages.

Arrived home about 9.30 p.m. and soon to bed.

11th August

Am keeping to my resolution. It is not so much of an effort, no smoke no alcohol and I am better I know. Tonight I go to

Talbot-Smith's to dine and discuss Surrey Shooting which means a longer dinner and late home I expect.

12th August

It was, arrived Chipstead 7.30 p.m. We had a very pleasant evening, I think we have saved the Surrey XX which might otherwise have been scrapped, as it had lost its identity.

21st August

To Bisley for Kent, Surrey and Hants annual match, Middlesex joining. Surrey won easily which means they have this year won everything they have entered. I shot very badly, being counted out for the first time in my life, must be either the gun or my eyes.

4th February 1939

My last entry was made over 17 months ago! And reading the last note as to self discipline it seems that I have not profited much by my effort. And yet there are excuses for not keeping it up as thoroughly as I started.

My Masonic Mastership of St Andrew's starting in February of last year meant a busy winter for me. Then I became President of the National Association of the Master Monumental Masons in May which since has taken much of my time. Also I was President of Farnham Rotary Club 1st July 1937 until 30th June 1938. This has meant very little spare time. So my diary has waited till now.

Reading through tonight my thoughts of a year and a half ago I realise there were some things I did not persevere with, smoking and alcohol lasted about three months. The thing that pleases me most is that I have kept my Sunday morning churchgoing up and have not missed many services since that day.

The war has loomed largely on the horizon. In September last it appeared that nothing could stop a war. The Prime

Minister did so however, but this year again it looks as though we shall not escape it for long.

19th February

I have thought today of the successive stages of family life. Our own childhood, with its interests and disappointments. Then the growing up, and dawning sense of responsibilities. The worries and anxieties of early manhood, and the struggle to make good.

Then the coming of the dear children with our life centred round them and the thought of their future. Watching them grow up with their worries and anxieties.

But what a tremendous amount of joy and happiness they bring. Then the realisation that they too have their own interests with others in their lives, and the thought that Mother and I are no longer their first consideration, and that we have reached a stage where we can watch and pray, but can do nothing further to influence them, and those happy childhood days are memories only.

And today the happy knowledge that with our grandchildren we start all over again, and shall have the joy of young children around to cheer and brighten the last stage of this mortal existence.

22nd February

Meeting arranged by J.J. Stevens and Mr Hopkins to discuss the formation of a Ratepayers Association in Farnham. We decided to call a public meeting on 6th March with a view to forming such an association and if decided upon to form a committee to act.

6th March

The meeting of the Ratepayers Association took place this evening and was an extraordinary event. The hall was crowded and people were being turned away before the opening time of eight o'clock. It was I think and everyone agreed an unqualified success. Hugh Edwards was good and undoubtedly helped tremendously. The provisional committee appointed seems a good one, and we are authorised to proceed with the formation of the Society at once.

24th March

Another crowded meeting of the Ratepayers Association, a committee was elected by ballot and we have at last got a Ratepayers association for Farnham and District. I was elected the first Chairman which I undertook for one year only.

3rd April

Going to Cornwall with Lorna and Joyce [daughters] for a holiday.

9th April, Easter Day

We all went to early service, eight o'clock at Falmouth Parish Church. The fullest communion service I have ever attended, must have been several hundred there.

April 16th

Church today at All Saints Church, Falmouth. My first experience of an Anglo Catholic service with full ritual ceremonial. Our time here draws to a close.

I have not written of the matter that is disturbing the whole world these days, but I believe God is watching and the trials of recent weeks will have the result of incalculable benefit to mankind once we all understand that very few are really bad at heart; and that the vast majority of the peoples of the earth want only to live in peace with their neighbours and only ask for a share of the good things of life.

12ᵗʰ March 1944

Five years since I wrote my last thoughts whilst in Falmouth with my girls.

I wrote in April 1939 that I believed God was watching, and presumed that the threats of war at that time were only trials. That we were to be allowed to sink back into the selfish, yet carefree lives most were living at that time.

God has punished me for that presumption, but he has brought me, I feel at last, nearer to him and to a realisation of the inner meaning of his goodness, charity and purpose.

War came after all in 1939, September 3ʳᵈ, horror commenced and I can only sketchily give after this long break, a few of the happenings since which have affected my life and the lives of those nearest and dearest to me.

All the boys were either called up or joined up in the Army at the outbreak. Everything was changed at once and can never be the same again.

17ᵗʰ March

Norman arrived home unexpectedly at about 11.15 p.m. having been to London for a medical examination.

Thank God he will be doing more useful work in his old unit, having his heart in it and nearly seven years training and experience.

He stayed the night and left at 10.30 a.m. He is well and full of cheerfulness and it was good to have him with us again, if for so short a time. Please God he may be successful in his efforts to get on, and I am hopeful. He deserves the best, being a tryer and always anxious to help others.

March 19ᵗʰ

I have been asked to take the chair at a Religious Life meeting, in the town during the week of 22ⁿᵈ April to 29ᵗʰ. I have agreed to do so but am a little doubtful of my qualifications for the task. I shall do my best by prayer beforehand to fit myself for the task and God will help me I know.

2nd April, Palm Sunday

A lot has happened since my last notes. Eric came home last Saturday evening and stayed till Monday when he left for Cornwall with Peg and the kiddies. He is surprisingly well but has obviously been very ill. Great happiness has reigned at home, and Mother is content having her boy home again.

Norman came in on Monday soon after Eric left, so just missed him, a great pity. He came back in the evening and stayed till Tuesday morning on his way back to the Isle of Wight. It was a duty trip and Norman is also well and happy.

12th April

Ten days since I wrote my last notes. I have spent eight happy days in Cornwall with Eric, Peggy, Lorna and their kiddies, and returned yesterday.

It was such a happy time after the agony and uncertainty following the War Office wire of 1st February. Eric is much better apart from being much thinner, and to be with him again in such happy surroundings was unbelievably wonderful.

Lorna too seems much happier, and is certainly better in health. She is now waiting for Penry to arrive from India.

We went to Church at St Enodock on Good Friday and Easter Sunday.

I feel convinced that most things will be very different for all of us, and if the world is to be a better place for struggling humanity, the old suspicions and animosities must be wiped out.

23rd April

This is a lovely spring so far, but for the War how much we could all enjoy it. I read the other day some well known person comments on spring in youth and spring in old age. Young people as a rule don't see all the beauty in early spring days. It is probably after a life of experience, the sorting out of the good from the dross, that one really sees the meaning—the real beauty of the wonderful spring days. I know for my own part they appeal to me more and more each year. Yesterday the drive on business to Whitchurch with Fred Alexander through peaceful Hampshire lanes was a thing of rest and contentment to me and made me very happy. I sat for some three hours enjoying the simple unspoilt beauty of the fields and lanes. Simple but bearing such wonderful and undeniable witness to the guiding and controlling hand in all natures glorious works.

26th April

Tonight I presided at the Religion in Industry meeting in the British Restaurant in connection with the towns Religion and Life week. I think the meeting was successful. The hall was filled with a gathering representing all classes and all denominations. I did my best and hope the words in my short opening remarks appealed to the audience. It was an ordeal because I have taken part and presided at many other kinds of social and industrial gatherings, I have never taken a leading part in a religious meeting of this sort.

14th May

Another break, which has been unavoidable. I am so tired and worn out most evenings that I simply haven't the strength left to concentrate on this writing.

Yesterday, a delightful day out with Ernie Langham, Joyce and the Surrey Archilogical Society around Guildford and Bramley. We found it very tiring owing to the unusual heat.

Today Ernie and I went to Communion at the little Compton Church, a cool spring morning and then on to a busy day with the Home Guard.

27th June

Over one month has passed. I find it impossible to write daily in present conditions. There is so much to do and I am a month older every month which under conditions of a terrible war finds one out.

I do not write of the war but such big things have happened since I last wrote here that I will refer to the opening of the Second Front in France with our invasion of Normandy and the capture of Cherbourg.

This with the Russians great successes in the East and our wonderful fellows in Italy, now well beyond Rome makes such a tremendous development that I do really believe that the war is now nearing the end. All over the world the end this year is freely spoken of, and I believe that this is not only possible but probable. God knows and will answer our prayers I am sure.

Farnham's Salute to Soldiers week ended last Saturday and the effort was a big and worthy one, over £210,000, this makes a notable contribution for a town of some 20,000 only.

After a very dry first half of the year we are getting rain at last. It is wanted badly for the crops and gardens, but is unfortunate for our fellows in France and for the haymaking, which I started on Sunday, the first day of the rain!

29th July

Eric, Peg, Lorna and the children have returned from Cornwall. Penry has been posted to the north of England and intends to have Lorna and David with him shortly.

Tom still at Clacton and gets to see us occasionally. Both good fellows, which is a comfort to Mother and I.

7th August, Bank Holiday

Spent a happy day with my family and during the afternoon toiled hard at the Y.M.C.A. fete (pony rides) at Farnham castle. Johnnie the pony did well here and we both arrived home late in the evening tired but happy.

10th August

Penry came home during the morning, and late in the evening left for the north again with Lorna and David. We have had Lorna and David home with us for some three weeks and home has been very bright in consequence. David is a darling and we shall miss him.

13th August

Norman rang up and asked Eric and I to go up to Chiswick to his Regt Sports on Wednesday. We are both going and I look forward to seeing him again with Eric.

Farnham Urban Council

Bert served on the Farnham Town Council for many years, being Chairman for three consecutive years (1951 – 1954) including the Coronation year.

A council memo from 1954 reports on a demonstration by a Reigate-based Food Flying Squad at Farnham, Surrey on 3rd March. Major H.C. Patrick, Chairman of the Council, is listed as one of those who inspected the vehicles.

> During the afternoon of Wednesday, 3rd March the Reigate-based Food Flying Squad was on display in the car park of the Council Offices, Farnham, for inspection by members of Farnham Civil Defence Welfare Section and members of the Council . . . The vehicles and equipment were described by Mr Periam, Assistant Ministry of Food Principal Emergency Officer, South Eastern Region, who explained the part these convoys would play in any peace-time or war-time emergency. Manned by their W.V.S. crews the convoys are ready to leave at short notice for the emergency site where they would serve hot food to the people until local emergency meals centres were organised.
>
> The convoys, which are stationed at strategic points throughout the country, consist of an office van, a 500 gallon water tanker, two stores vans and four canteen vans, and are

designed to act as the spearhead of emergency feeding. This convoy has already been in action in Canterbury in 1942, Dover in 1944, and the Kent floods in 1953, and these 'battle honours' are recorded on the side of each van.

The convoys carry their own Soyer boilers for boiling water and making soups and stews. But an alternative and useful way of obtaining boiling water was demonstrated at Farnham Dairy, Weydon Lane, when the steam sterilising jets were used to heat water in the tea urns. The urns from the convoy were filled with cold water at the dairy. A steam jet rapidly brought it to boiling point, the tea infusers were lowered into the boiling water and the tea was then ready for transport to the site if the emergency. After watching this demonstration at the dairy, members of the Council and C.D. Welfare Section were served with cups of tea from one of the convoy vans at the Council Offices.

HERBERT'S OTHER OFFICIAL ROLES AND INTERESTS

He was Chairman of the Trimmers Hospital Committee for many years.

He was Church Warden for several years, and was a Freemason.

He was delighted to be appointed Deputy Lieutenant of the county of Surrey on the 28th November 1955.

He died in his sleep peacefully at his beloved Gwanda on 12th December 1966.

Editor's postscript:

For several years Bert, in the late 1940s, took his male grandchildren on a one week holiday to Wales with one of his daughters to help him. They had a wonderful time. Every year I petitioned him that *next year* it would be the *girls'* turn. Every year I was promised that indeed this is just what would happen. Sadly it was boys only every year.

Bert as Deputy Lieutenant of Surrey. At Gwanda,
Old Compton Lane, Farnham.

ERNEST

ERNEST HENRY PATRICK

**Written by Ernest's friend, Arthur J. Wheeler, who,
until the entries for 1945, writes in Ernest's voice**

The diary opens as Ernest prepares to leave Farnham, Surrey, for Canada. With him is his friend Arthur ('Art').

1904

25th April

Went up to Farnham Park with Nipper [Harold] and played football with him for the last time.

26th April

Farewell party with old chums. Sugar Varney, Fred Guest, Charlie Porter and Jeremy Herglies.

27th April

Getting ready to start. Missed train, but left home for Waterloo 3.57. Went to Aunt Nell Chittendens, Lincoln's Inn.

Aunt and Uncle accompany us to Euston Station, leaving for Liverpool 12 p.m.

28th April

Arrived at Liverpool six o'clock. Changed money, had our last breakfast in old England for a time.

Got tickets, arrived at Docks went off in tender 'Skirmisher' to Allan Line 'Bavarian'. Got our berth numbers: three and four in Room 45. Watched baggage come aboard, then to dinner consisting of soup, beef and potatoes.

Four o'clock: 'Bavarian' went alongside landing stage to take on saloon passengers. Many people to see us off at 5.30 p.m., when we sailed on the great adventure, bidding farewell to old England.

Went below and had tea, corned beef, bread and butter and jam.

Going on deck found weather rough, both feeling not quite the thing.

Nine o'clock climbed into our bunks. Slept soundly till five next morning feeling OK.

29th April

Had our first wash since leaving Farnham. Went on deck, rolling a bit. Breakfast 7.30 a.m. Bloaters, bread and butter and marmalade and coffee. Now laying off the Irish Coast at Moville.

Two tenders come alongside with more passengers and mail. We sent two letters back by one hawker. Then had dinner: soup, beef, fish, potatoes, stewed apples and rice. Sailed again at two o'clock.

Feeling a bit queer and at 3.15 p.m. fed the fishes. Lost sight of land 5.30 p.m. Art seasick at 7.30 p.m. Went below, slept fairly well till morning.

30th April

Didn't feel like getting up, so lay in our bunks all day. No meals but had to keep getting up to feed fishes. Seas rolling tremendously. Went out for tea, ate some bread and pickles then to bunks till morning.

1st May, Sunday

Still have a piece of bread and sausages brought from Farnham. Went up on deck and had our first smoke since Friday.

Seas rough, wind bitterly cold, didn't stay long, but retreat to our bunks. Church Services and Concert were held but too groggy to join them.

Went down to the ladies lavatory and had a good wash. Have to get up early and get there before the ladies rise.

Just sighted a ship homeward bound, first since leaving Ireland. Then to breakfast, stew and potatoes, bread and marmalade.

Went up on deck, sea calmer, went aft and had a game of deck quoits. Then went below to give up passage tickets.

Dinner: more stew.

On deck had another game of quoits, me and Art against two other fellows. Twenty-one up, of course Farnham won. Spent the rest of the afternoon reading old letters. Went below for tea, couldn't drink the stuff they called tea (tea and soup mixed) so had soda water 3d a bottle, then turned into our bunks.

3rd May

Woke to find the sea rough, ship rolling tremendously.

Breakfast: curry and rice, rotten bread, marmalade and butter. (Marmalade the best food item.) This day the cook's ears must have burned to a cinder.

Ate the last two Farnham sausages and started one of the cakes, very nice. Had Dinner: more stew, haricot beans, tapioca and jam.

Had another turn on deck, too rough to stay long. Today has been the roughest we have had so far, waves mountainous, wind a hurricane.

Tea time came round, but did not have any. Went up on deck again. On returning Art slipped on the wet deck and slid on his back down hatchway steps to the bottom. Retired for the night.

4th May

Woke up just after 4 a.m., had a wash and then heard a cry. All hands on deck to see the iceberg, so went up and saw the seas rolling a lot. We are looking some pretty beauties now, haven't had a scrape since leaving home.

Just had breakfast, best yet. Minced meat of some sort. Have got over seasickness, are in the best of condition.

Have had our first shave at sea, and wasn't it cold afterwards. Managed the operation without cutting ourselves.

Sighted two more icebergs, weather beautiful, stayed on deck all morning. Dinner: soup beef and Plum Duff which we enjoyed.

Tea: Corned beef, bread and blackberry jam. Enjoyed our meals today, went aft to smoking room feeling tip top now. Farnham cake is gradually diminishing.

There has been the death of a baby. Lowered overboard eight o'clock.

Slept well but was awakened in the middle of the night with a cry 'All hands on deck to see the iceberg'. The idiot was soon chased back to his bunk.

5th May

Rose at 5.30 a.m. Had a good wash. Writing letters home till breakfast time.

Breakfast: steak, marmalade. Resumed writing. Were examined for vaccination and passed.

Dinner: soup, mutton, rice and prunes. Turned on deck and sighted land at 1.45 p.m. also some fishing vessels.

Newfoundland most likely. From twelve o'clock yesterday to twelve today travelled 374 miles.

Tea: Pigs feet etc. Then a sing song and concert. Turned in.

6th May

Went up on deck, land still in sight but had to slow down on account of floating ice. Enjoyed a smoke then below for breakfast. Bread, butter and marmalade.

Have been lying off Cape Kay, Newfoundland since breakfast, signalling to the station on shore, to know whether we can go down the St Laurence on to Halifax. Coast very bleak hereabouts.

Weather beautiful, had supper, biscuits and coffee. Then went aft and had a chat with the look out man. The liner 'Lake Champlain' is lying about half a mile away, hove to, waiting for us to lead the way through the ice floes.

We are going to Quebec. We start again at 5.30 but very slowly, soon come to a stop for the night. Ice floes very heavy, smashing alongside.

Passengers aboard 1800, crew 365, and there are 124 stewards on the 'Bavarian'.

After a concert turned in and slept well.

7ᵗʰ May

Turned out 6.30 a.m., weather grand. Had a smoke, then breakfast.

Lot of ice around, proceeding slowly. Can see footprints in the snow on the floes and seals in the distance.

Getting into thicker ice now. It is a sight to see nothing but snow and ice. Dinner: two potatoes, soup, tapioca and jam.

1.30 p.m., cleared the ice and went into the smoothest water I have ever seen, expect we are in the mouth of the St Laurence. Just passed an island and some big rocks. We passed through 45 miles of ice in ten hours. Had tea then went aft where dancing was in full swing to the sound of violins and bagpipes. Went below at ten o'clock.

8ᵗʰ May

Had breakfast, then had our boots cleaned, charge one cent. Turned our collars inside out, so are looking a little more respectable.

We are now passing down the St Laurence, land visible both sides. French Canadian farms dotted about. Villages look pretty with gaily painted houses and churches. Had a turn on saloon deck, where it was warmer. Saw the Allan liner 'Dorian' pass on her way home.

Have been seeing about our luggage. Expect to land early tomorrow.

Dinner and tea as usual, turning in at ten o'clock, but went up on deck two or three times to see if Quebec was in sight.

About two o'clock woken up by a lot of noise, so turned out on deck. Found we were alongside dock at Quebec, baggage being unloaded. All passengers ordered below.

9th May

Had breakfast 4.30 a.m. then landed, our feet touching Canadian soil five o'clock. Went to the Immigration Hall where we passed 'Doctor', and got our tickets stamped. Then we went grub hunting and got:

3 loaves of bread 15 cents

2 lbs German sausage 25 cents

2 lbs cheese 30 cents

1 lb sugar 5 cents

4lbs biscuits 40 cents

We left Quebec at one o'clock for Winnipeg. Made friends on the train with two Cornish fellows. One named Short and the other named Day.

Had a great time on the train playing Tip it, and helping Short dispose of Cornish home-made cooking.

Our beds were very hard, we laid on our coats with a rug for a pillow. At train stops we stretched our legs and got some wood for the stove. Everybody having to do their own cooking. Got out at North Bay and bought some more grub. Rough country, forest and rock in this section.

12th May

Arrived Winnipeg 4.30, went to Immigration Hall. Then up main street, where we saw the Union Bank Building being erected. Very tall steel framework.

Red River mud much in evidence.

Left same day for Brandon, but got out at Portage la Prairie at 9.30.

Got a job with a farmer, Charles Lytte of High Bluff. Wages 12.50 per month each. I went out with him, Art stayed in town until the 16th May when Mr Lytte brought him out to the farm.

Weather very hot, hard job rolling out at 4.30 and working till late at night.

1st June

We are getting hardened, but had sore hands with blisters, sore feet and muscles for a while.

6th July

Both of us turned barber, cutting each other's hair. Did a fair job.

12th July

Holiday. Boss and family went away for the day. We hoisted a Union Jack, a small one we had brought with us. Glad of a rest for the day.

6th August

Had chicken for dinner.

25th August

Boss started cutting Wheat. We were stooking.

September

Stacking wheat with a man in the field pitching. Art and I pitched 30 loads a day on the stacks.

Completing three 10-load stacks. How our feet and muscles ached. Socks soaking wet and feet raw, we vowed that as soon as we had the necessary dollars we would book our passages home.

Wages for harvest 15 dollars a month each.

Art staying at Lyttes all winter.

10th November

Art leaves today to work for Ed Childs, an old country man whose wife has just come out from London. He will be about a mile away.

28th November

Very stormy, snowing and freezing hard. Our first experience of a Canadian winter.

Christmas Day

Art came up and had dinner and stayed all afternoon.

27th December

Art fell down cellar at Childs and nearly broke his neck.

1905

1st January, New Year's Day

Went down to Childs and had dinner. Turkey and Plum Pudding.

10th January

Art and I had the team and sleigh. Went to Portage shopping.

13th January

Took part in a concert at Dale school. Went to bed at 2.30 a.m.

16th January

Went to Literary meeting at Dale School. Glorious night, Northern Lights grand.

8th February

Terrible blizzard.

10th March

Went down to Ed Childs. About 30 people there. Cards and dancing till 2.30 a.m.

31st March

Concert at Dale School, took part in Dialogue. Won by strategy.

7th April

Went to Portage.

12th April

Left Lyttes went to work for Cramptons. Heard Bert [his brother] is going to South Africa.

27th April

Talking to a man working on the next farm, found he was from Bentley. Tom Vickery by name. Curious as this is the first anniversary of our leaving home.

24th May

Bitterly cold day.

31ˢᵗ May

Mosquitoes bad.

29ᵗʰ June

Went to Prospect picnic to play for Dale baseball team. Terrible accident, man fatally injured running into telephone pole in horse race.

30ᵗʰ June

Went to Dale picnic, had ice cream and bananas.

11ᵗʰ July

Bad thunderstorm.

25ᵗʰ July

Art, George Dixon, and Bob Moggies and I went to Winnipeg Exhibition by train had a good time.

10ᵗʰ September

Went out duck shooting with some of the boys. Cleaned and roasted duck. One a piece. Had a sing song, got home 1 a. m.

26ᵗʰ October

Froze up.

19ᵗʰ November

Had our photo taken at Portage.

23ʳᵈ December

Went down to visit Art, and broke a bottle of Port.

Christmas Eve

Went down to Art's again, stayed all night.

Christmas Day

Went to Moggies for dinner and enjoyed ourselves.

1906

10th January

Art, I and Alec Ingram went to Portage to see an ice hockey game for the first time. A great game, very fast. On the way home saw an accident, sleigh turned upside down. Went and helped, man's wrist broken.

3rd February

Art had a mishap, badly damaging knee cap, so went down and bathed the knee.

March

We are talking of going to Sheho, Saskatchewan to file for a homestead.

9th April

Charlie Lytte took me, Art and Billie Lovell into High Bluff, where we caught train to Portage and stayed the night.

10th April

Having heard that homesteads were available in the Sheho country, we took train for Yorkton at l0 a.m., arriving there at 7.30 p.m.

Slept at Balmoral Hotel.

11th April

Saw the Govt agent of lands and got map of homesteads. Then struck out on Shanks Pony for Sheho 42 miles away, along the railroad track. Trains only running twice weekly.

Arrived at Theodore at eight o'clock, having covered 25 miles in $5^1/_2$ hours. Found we could get neither food, drink nor a bed, so went supperless, and slept in an unfinished Hotel on the bare floor.

12th April

This morning had a hard job to get breakfast, but finally persuaded a crabby old lady to provide. Then struck out for Sheho, 17 miles, arrived in time for supper at the Dacobale Hotel.

13th April

Lovell and I struck out for Foam Lake on a search for homesteads. Art staying in Sheho, his knee having played out.

After travelling all round the Ladstock district (walking) some 50 miles from Sheho, and meeting some old country people, Andrew Fudge from Portsmouth, Bill Hutchinson from London, we arrived back at Sheho.

17th April

We had picked on three homesteads. Put numbers in a hat and drew. Art and I drew the homesteads adjoining. Lucky!

Left for Yorkton by train at 3 p.m.

18th April

Went to the Land Office and filed on our homesteads.

19th April

Took train to Portage again, arrived at 5.30. Got a job at George Lytte's, father of Charles.

September

Had a farewell party at Dales Farm. Eleven of us, all bachelors. Did our own cooking, three turkeys and all the trimmings. Broke up early in the morning.

15th October

After saying goodbye to the folks, left Portage for Yorkton, arriving 7.30. Slept at the Balmoral Hotel.

16th October

Left for Sheho, and waited there for Bill Hutchinson till the 18th. He did not arrive, so started walking to Ladstock, which we reached at 7.30, (30 miles).

Had supper and bed at Andrew Fudge's.

19th October

Started for our homesteads, arriving at Pat Thorpe's, a bachelor farmer, at 10.30 a.m. Stayed till Monday 22nd, when Bill Hutchinson with a yoke of oxen and wagon got back with a load of our goods.

23rd October

Went over to my homestead. During the summer, Pat had built a log cabin on each homestead. Size 16 feet by 14 feet with a lumber roof, one door and one window.

When we arrived we had to clunk the walls, that is fill spaces between logs with pieces of wood and then plaster the seams.

Got a fire going, we rolled up on our blankets, but pretty chilly on our first day's residence on land of my own.

24th October

Clunking and plastering.

25th October

Clunking and plastering.

26th October

Digging well.

27th October

Bill Hutchinson arrived with our load of supplies from Sheho, 40 miles away. Cleaned up shanty and cooked a couple of rabbits for dinner, Billy Lovell baking buns.

Snowing. Went in the bush cutting poles to make table legs and bedstead.

2nd November

Made a table and shelves.

28th November

Bought a quarter of beef, 128 lbs at $3^1/_2$ per lb.

19th December

Went to Ladstock for mail.

24th December

Chopped up a pile of wood. Took our guns and took a stroll over my homestead. Got back and found 'old country' mail brought by Billy. Just right for Xmas.

Art and I are backing together.

25th December, Christmas Day

When we rose we found it snowing and storming. Started our Xmas Dinner at 20 to 1. Consisted of Roast Beef, Yorkshire Pudding, potatoes and turnips and lastly Xmas Pudding all put up first class bachelor style.

26th December

We went over to Mr Ruxton's, a neighbour, a sea captain hailing from Liverpool, to a dance, trudging through two feet of snow. Broke up at dawn.

31st December, New Years Eve

Went over to Jock McWalter's, a Scot, much like Harry Lauder.

1907

1st January, New Years Day

We all went over to Jock's to celebrate New Year. Seven other fellows were there, another bachelor party. Had a fine dinner, Roast prairie chicken, beans, potatoes, apple pie and Xmas pudding, then played cards.

9th January

Mr Ruxton came over and hauled up two loads of wood. On the road saw fine deer.

13th January

Went over to Bovaird's, an Irish family, had a good time.

14th January

Went over to Ruxton's, played cards till midnight, then tramped home on snow shoes. Bitterly cold, got my heels frozen, so on arriving home put on a big fire in the stove. Next thing the roof was burning so had to move fast and put it out.

18th January

My birthday, Mr and Mrs Ruxton, Mrs James and Billy Lovell came over and spent the day.

8th February

Bill Hutchinson came over and hauled out firewood and 20 logs.

10th February

Went to Ladstock for mail.

13th February

Bill Hutchinson hauled out 24 logs.

15th February

Hauled out 33 logs.

16th February

Building stables.

18th February

Same.

19th February

Finished stables.

21st February

Started Art's stables.

2nd March

Finished Art's stables.

15th March

Bad blizzard.

17th March

Went to Church Service at McKenney's.

Ernest's first cabin

Ernest's house, built 1918.

18th March

Another bad storm, much snow.

21st March

Another bad storm and snow.

24th March

Went to Church Service.

7th April

Went to Church Service.

10th April

Snowing again.

13th April

Went to Sheho with Bill Hutchinson.

17th April

Got back from Sheho four o'clock. Long trip with the oxen.

20th April

Barbering.

21st April

Church service.

5th May

Church service.

14th May

Bill Hutchinson came over and seeded my breaking new land. Art and I were plastering shanty with lime and sand mortar.

16th May

Shot two ducks.

21st May

Raining, washing clothes.

22nd May

We started fencing crop land with poplar rails.

27th May

Finished fencing.

30th May

Started out looking for work. Walked about 40 miles.

Started work with the Canadian White Construction Company on construction of road bed of the new Canadian National Railway.

There are six camps working at different places within a few miles all under canvas. There are about 30 teams of horses in a camp. We are No 5 camp.

Met quite a lot of 'old country' fellows who are coming out to work on this job. Met a Jim Hale from Hale, and a fellow named Bugler from Alton.

Art has moved to No 6 camp where he is running the dump-on grader on a big fill across a lake. See him often.

July

About a dozen of us, old country fellows, including a Welshman, took a ramble on the Prairie one Sunday evening and climbed to the top of a big hill. There was a lake on the west side, the sun was just setting, and the reflection in the water was red. We stood for a while admiring the scene, then we all broke into the Glory Song, unforgettable as the echoes rolled over the hills.

This is the Touchwood Hills district. There is an old Hudson Bay port near, on the old Telegraph Trail. Numerous Indian reserves here. The Gordon, Day Star and Muskswegan, mostly Cree Indians.

One day Art heard a fellow yelling at his team in the camp, thought he recognised the voice, and discovered it was Bill Fortesque from Farnham.

It's a fine life under canvas but now it's November it gets pretty chilly. Our bedsteads are stakes driven in the ground, cross pieces and poles nailed on and straw on top.

15th November

Finished up. Headed for home 30 miles, with heavy loads of blankets and gear on our backs. Arrived at a neighbour bachelor's at dark, played out. Just laid flat on the floor and went to sleep.

18th November

Went to Sheho.

21st November

Arrived home at 3 a.m. Bought a yoke of oxen from Bill Hutchinson for 85 dollars.

9th December

Bought a wagon for 16 dollars.

10th December

Fixing up Art's shanty.

31st December, New Years Eve

Had a party.

1908

21st January

Art went to Kelleher and saw the first train pull in laying steel.

24th February

Went to Farrar's. We have been cutting logs all winter.

9th March

Building granary.

12th March

Went to Farrar's and Lizzie says 'yes'. [Ernest had made a marriage proposal to Lizzie Jane Farrar.]

15th March

Arrived home again with mail.

16th March

Building granary.

18th March

Billy Lovell shot a wolf today.

26th March

Grand display of Northern Lights.

One night this winter saw two black faces looking in at the window. Black faces with white stripes going down the back. Didn't know what animals they were so went out with the rifle and chased them, but they disappeared in the dark. Good job I didn't catch up with them as I have since found out they are skunks.

11th April

Finished putting roof on granary.

13th April

Started for Sheho. Prairie fires all round.

17th April

Arrived back from Sheho.

24th April

Awful snow storm.

7th May

Art started for Sheho where he met Frank [his brother]. They came out to Farrar's and stayed all night.

9th May

Walked from there getting home at five o'clock.

16th June

Came home from Sheho where I have been working and playing football. Art has been breaking up more land. Now I have to start.

17th June

Breaking.

29th June

Frank and Art left to work on the Canadian National Railway, ballasting and laying steel.

15th November

They came home again.

30th November

Frank and I went down to Farrar's.

1st December

Working with Art helping heaving logs for a house.

8th December

Started building.

12th December

Finished walls.

13th December

Frank and I went to services.

24th December

Frank, Art and I walked to Farrar's.

25th December

Enjoyed our Xmas very much.

28th December

Bad storm.

1909

Working in Foam Lake all winter.

3rd April

Went up to homestead. Art and Frank putting roof on my house.

April till July

Playing football for Foam Lake till July when Lizzie and I were married at Edmore, later coming out to the homestead to settle down to farming.

In the meanwhile Art and Frank had gone working on the Canadian National Railway. Later during this year we bought: a new wagon, a Binder and plough.

1910

I bought sleighs, three cows and a horse and buggy.

Elsie was born this year.

1st December

Art came up from the railroad and stayed until 8th December when I took him to Lestock en route to England, going by way of Minneapolis, Chicago, Toronto, Montreal and St Johns New Brunswick, arriving at St Johns, 14th December.

16th December to 23rd December

Art sailed on 'Empress of Britain' to Liverpool and home once more on Xmas Eve.

1911

Harry born this year.
 This year I bought a team of horses, Baldy and George.

24th March

Art went and saw Grandmother Patrick.

29th March

Art went at midnight for Nurse Phillips [midwife]. A son born to Ted and Min Wheeler on 30th March.

4th April

Art went to Bert Patrick's and spent the evening. Art took Harold [Ernest's little brother] over to see Mr and Mrs Croucher [Bert, Ernest and Harold's Grandparents], and said goodbye to them. Harold very interested in soldiers on manoeuvres.

12th April

Art went and saw Bert again.

19th April

Art went and said goodbye to Pa Patrick, then he left Farnham for Canada, both our Dads came to see him off.
 Arriving at Waterloo Station he went to Lincoln's Inn Fields and stayed with Aunt Nell, Uncle Fred and Nellie, and Aunt Min who walked with him to Euston and saw him off. Farmer Cudby travelling with him.

20th April

Art sailed from Liverpool on 'SS Montrose' and arrived in Form Lake on 9th May where I met him, driving out to Farrar's in the pouring rain.

10th May

We arrived back home.

22nd May

Art and I went to Foam Lake then to Wynyard for Coronation Day celebrations.

22nd June

I played football for Foam Lake, then breaking more land for 2 weeks.

July

Hay making.

21st August

Killing pig, amateur butchers.

4th September

Started cutting wheat.

4th November

Finished stacking grain, it snowed all night.

6th December

Steam threshing machine moved in, had to use snow plough so the outfit could move

7th and 8th December

Threshing.

Wheat price 50 cents
Oat price 30 cents

25th December, Christmas Day

Art came along.

1912

14th January

Received Xmas mail.

30th January

Went to Foam Lake.

9th April

Started seeding wheat.

30th June

Went to Form Lake. Terrible cyclone in Regina.

13th July

Art and I went to Foam Lake and played football for Foam Lake against Yorkton. Foam Lake winning 8 – 1. Arrived home 1.30 a.m.

26th July

Went to Sheho.

17th August

Cutting wheat at Art's place.

30th September

Started stacking wheat. Very wet fall. Didn't finish till 30th November. Didn't get threshed till Christmas.
1912 Crop prices
Wheat 50 cents a bushel
Oats 20 cents a bushel.

1913

Nellie born this year.

5th January

Very cold, 46 degrees below.

6th January

Very cold, 40 degrees below.

8th January

Art brought team of horses.

22nd January

Hauling wheat to Leross. 15 miles.

23rd to 30th January

Ditto.

30th January

A bad wind, nearly 40 below. Just about frozen when I got home.

11th February

Hauling wheat 40 below.

12th and 13th February

Ditto.

This has been a bad winter, very stormy, very cold and trails bad. Hauling grain every day is no snap. Start on the road 5a.m. Get home in the dark. Load up again for next day and do chores. Go to bed for a while, get up at 3 a.m., off again at 5 a.m.

11th April

Snow all gone.

18th April

Started seeding.

28th May

Finished.

6th July

All wheat headed out.

20th August

Started cutting wheat and barley.

1st November

Started threshing.

5th November

Finished threshing.

8th November

Trapping musk rats.

10th November

Trapping musk rats.
Trapped 32.

25th December, Christmas Day

Spent a quiet time.

31st December

Jimmy Farrar came along.

1914

1st January, New Year's Day

Nice New Year's Day.
Played football.

1915

17th January

Art and Ed Ruxton gone to the University of Saskatoon, taking a short course in agriculture.

22nd to 24th January

Very cold, 40 degrees below.

12th April

Seeding wheat.

16th June

Finished digging new well.

25th August

Started cutting wheat.

16th September

Finished cutting grain.

15th October

Started threshing.
1912 Crop prices: Wheat 50 cents a bushel
1913 Crop prices: Wheat 65 – 70 cents a bushel
1914 Crop prices: Wheat 90cents – 1 dollar a bushel
1915 Crop prices: Wheat 1 dollar a bushel

1916

January

Very cold all month.

23rd June

Art putting in concrete foundation of his house.

8th July

Carpenters out.

26th July

Finished his house.

28th July

Art gone to Winnipeg to meet his missus to be.

29th July

Arrived in the Peg and stayed with Mr and Mrs Harry Snowden. He went and saw Ern Whittington, formerly of Farnham.

1st August

Art went to the station and met Min, who was accompanied by Miss Preston of Leeds who was coming out to be married to Harry Beanland, one of our near neighbours.

3rd August

Art was married in Winnipeg and arrived back here on 5th August.

11th October

Threshing again.
1916 Crop prices:
Wheat 1.50 a bushel
Oats 40 cents a bushel

1917

1st February

Coldest day of winter, 40 degrees below.

28th July

A daughter born to Art and Min, named Doris.

8th October

Threshing again.

25th to 29th October

Snowing, froze up.

1st November

Thawing out.

2nd to 24th November

Started to plough. Lovely weather, no frost at night. NB This was the warmest and loveliest November in 43 years.

10th December

Have the telephone installed.

25th to 28th December

Christmas Day and following mighty cold, 40 below.

1917 Crop prices:
Wheat 1.98 a bushel
Oats 71 cents a bushel

1918

Built a new house.

Allenby School district was formed, and a school was built and opened in August. I, being one of the Trustees at this time, suggested the school be named Allenby as the name of Field Marshall Allenby was much in the news at this time. This name was adopted.

Elsie, Harry and Nellie all received their education at Allenby.

11th November: PEACE DECLARED.

1918 Crop prices:

Wheat 1.90 a bushel
Oats 60cents a bushel

1919

Went to a meeting [17th May 1919], called for the purpose of forming a local lodge of the Sask Grain Growers association. Appointed Vice President.

A dry summer.
1919 Crop prices:
Wheat 1.92 a bushel
Oats 72 cents a bushel

1920

15th March

Terrible blizzard from the north. Snow drifts 14 feet to 20 feet deep.

30th September

Threshing.

3rd November

Digging well.

8th November

Froze up.
1920 Crop prices:
Wheat 1.60 a bushel
Oats 30 cents a bushel.

1921

January

Went to Moose Jaw.

1924

Delegate at Sask Grain Growers Convention.
   Took part in the organisation of the Saskatchewan Wheat Pool.
   Was President of the Lestock Wheat Pool Committee for three years, 1925 1926 1927.

1927

A branch of the C P Railway being constructed from Foam Lake, will pass about $4^1/_2$ miles north of here.

August

Gangs at work at Bank End building grade. Hauling grain to Bank End.

1928

A local committee of the Saskatchewan Wheat Pool was formed at Bank End. I was a member for some years. Art was secretary for 13 years. The President of the Saskatchewan Wheat Pool was Alex Mc Phail a local man who homesteaded in the Bank End district in the early days.

1929

Start of the great depression of the 1930s. Prices of all agricultural products going down.

1930

Prices still dropping.

Ernest, Nellie, Lizzie and Harry.

Ernest and Lizzie, in her flower garden.

Wheat 30 cents a bushel
Oats 10 cents a bushel
Beef 2 to 3 cents a lb on the hoof
Eggs 8 cents a dozen

1933

The southern part of the province dried out.

A meeting was called in Bank End and a committee formed of which I was Chairman. Everybody went to work, to help and loaded 45,000 lbs of potatoes, all for free, which were sent to Big Beaver.

1934

A cooperative oil refinery was organised in Regina for the purpose of manufacturing and supplying Petroleum products to Saskatchewan farmers. This was the first Co operative Refinery in the world.

1936

I was elected a member of the Emerald Municipal Council for Division 2.

1937

This year will always be remembered for the terrible drought in Western Canada. Practically no rain since the snow melted. Grass hoppers and caterpillars eating up what little green stuff there is left. Crop about six inches high, headed out, much of it burnt dry. Saskatchewan may harvest enough for seed and feed.

5th July

The hottest day ever recorded in Canada, 114 degrees, which followed weeks of temperatures around 100 degrees.

This day, 5th July, was terrible and culminated in a destructive storm or twister which struck two miles east of here. Houses were torn off the foundations and reduced to matchwood. Hail lay 14 inches deep on the ground. A granary with 300 bushels of wheat in it was picked up by the wind and disappeared.

1938

These days a councillor's job is not a happy one. There is a lot of work to be done in the organisation and distribution of relief in the way of goods and clothing. Hay and feed grain to be shipped in from Manitoba and distributed.

Some 800,000 people in Western Canada are being provided for by the Government as a result of the crop failure.

1939

May

The King and Queen came to Canada.

The effects of the drought and low prices are still in evidence.

Wheat 60 cents a bushel. Farmers up in arms in protest.

7th August

The Bank End Co operative Association incorporated. I am on the Board of Directors.

3rd September

WAR AGAIN

December

Resigned as councillor.

1940

Price of wheat 77 cents a bushel. Compared with what a farmer has to buy, this price is ruinous.

Another farmer's Co operative has been formed: The Canadian Co-operative Implements, also a Co operative Flour Mill.

I am appointed President of the Bank End Co-operative and Art appointed secretary.

1941

Price of wheat 74 cents.

1942

Due to low price of wheat, 400 Delegates bearing a petition signed by 185,000 farmers are en route to Ottawa to present the petition to the Government.

Result: price of wheat raised to 90 cents.

Crop good this year. Again President of the Co Op.

1943

January

Art's boy Edgar reported for military service.

I was appointed president Co Op again. Crop good.

1944.

Price of wheat increased to 1.05. Great scarcity of labour on the farms.

Appointed president of Co Op again. Crops good. Edgar leaving for overseas.

1945

Appointed President of Co Op. Crops good.

For the remaining entries, Arthur Wheeler speaks in his own voice:

This diary has been written in appreciation of a lifelong friendship begun in 1900 at Farnham, Surrey, and ending on August 24th 1945.

1945

Ern came over to see me and we talked about binder repairs. I am going to his place and looking at his binders, when he has made a list and told me what repairs were needed. We also talked about Co Op business. I left him about four o'clock. But it was not for us to know that it was our last meeting.

24th August

Alan and I were fixing our binder when Harry came over and said his Dad had been killed by the bull. I went immediately with him, with the hope that he still lived, but found him at peace. We lifted him into the car and brought him home.

26th August

The funeral service was held on Sunday 26th August 1945. The remains being laid to rest in Bank End Cemetery.

And thus ended a life lived to the fullest in a vocation of which he had vision when he wrote to me 23rd February 1903 from Oxford, and about which we had often talked on our rambles through Moor Park, Compton and particularly Farnham Park, where we spent many happy hours at the cricket nets and football.

Memories of these days are a priceless treasure, because there is today a gap that can never be filled.

After sharing in all the ups and downs, the rough with the smooth for 45 years, I still and shall always miss the opportunity to talk things over now; with the hope that these few notes will give an insight of the long trek down through the years and that it will be a keepsake for you, Violet.

I close this book.

Notes from Arthur Wheeler's diary of life in Camp 5 and 6 (Ernest stayed in Camp 5)

On 30th May Ernest, Billy Lovell and I left our homesteads, walking through Horse Lake district to a point on the G.T.P. [Grand Trunk Pacific] railway, now known as Kelliher, looking for construction work. From there we walked west up the right of way till we came to a Canadian White Construction Company, a few miles east of Punnichy where we secured jobs at No 5 Camp.

Probably every homesteader from a wide area was employed. Their numbers augmented by relays of old country immigrants brought out by ship load by a man named Short. Freighters transported the men and supplies from Lipton and always had wagon loads of men to take back, the loneliness and mosquitoes proving too much for many of them. At that time water levels were high – every slough and lake was full so that before construction could be started water had to be drained off. It was digging ditches, while being tormented by millions of mosquitoes, that most of the newly arrived immigrants were employed. Hundreds of them just worked until the next freighter arrived and then packed up. All the construction work was done with horses and mules, wheelers and scrapers. The only occasion on which mechanical means were used was in 1906, when a steam shovel was brought in to widen a cut east of Punnichy.

When a new camp was being formed, I was transferred to No. 6 where for several months I ran the dump on a big fill across a lake near the Indian Mission. On completion of the fill to the centre of the lake we moved camp to the east side. Then on completion of this section we moved westward to what is now Touchwood siding passing a store kept by Henry Fisher, then turning in near the Hudson Bay Post. We didn't proceed far before we had to unload a plow to turn furrows on a side hill to enable the loaded wagons to pass without turning over.

Shortly before reaching the camp site a lovely scene unfolded on the west side of the track. We saw through the trees a large lake dotted with tiny islands and around the islands hundreds of pelicans floated.

Arriving at the camp site we found two other camps in the vicinity. There were over a hundred teams assembled within a quarter of a mile to complete the last link, a bad stretch of small knolls and deep potholes. One other camp had to close down losing most of their horses to glanders.

We commenced work on a small knoll with thirteen teams and scrapers. Two of us worked on the dumps and got no rest as the teams were coming in a continuous circle. Opposite to us was a mule outfit. Since the scraper had to be dumped sideways into the water it was hard to get the mules close enough to the edge of the dump, so the boss stood in the centre and batted the nearest mule with a shovel. Sometimes the team went overboard. A watch was never needed for within a few minutes of 12 o'clock the mules would stop and bray. The cook used to dump refuse on the side of the slough and at night on approaching the water hundreds of 'plops' could be heard, made by muskrats; there must have been thousands along the right of way.

It was a great life under canvas, The Company provided the best of food, and the men were well treated. The men provided their own amusements. For beds we drove four posts into the ground, nailed slats on and stole some hay. When the weather became cold the bull cook, an old country Scots Guards drill sergeant possessed of a vile temper had to have fires going in the tents when the boys finished work. Whether there was a fire going or not we would complain loudly to get his goat. Scottie was usually within earshot and emerging from one tent or another would roar in his best parade ground manner, grab a cordwood stick and the boys would have to fly!

Finally we completed the grade on the G.T.P. on 14th November 1907. On 15th November I struck out on foot from Touchwood Siding with $207.50 in my pocket. (Wages were $40 dollars a month and board.) I was loaded with a heavy pack, (clothes, blankets, two loaves of bread, a big hunk of cheese and a dollar bottle of vanilla) but did not reach my shack. After travelling 25 miles in 6 hours, I stopped at a bachelor's shack, stretched out on the floor, pack on my back and went to sleep.

On 29th June 1908 I resumed railroading on the G.T.P. ballasting and laying the track, working from Semans to Jasmin. We had forty or fifty Doukhobors in the gang and occasionally they would give me the Sunday job of writing out an order to Eaton's for their requirements. Their diet consisted largely of eggs and the Raymore farmers were unable to keep up with their demand. The gang was composed of all nationalities, British, Italians, French, Romanians, Ukrainians, Jews and Negro. The camp was never free of vermin, the hay in our bunks had to be discarded and for many months we slept on bare boards. Meat was kept fresh by sprinkling quarters of beef and hog carcasses with pepper and hoisting them to the top of high poles sunk in the ground.

That November I came home with $118.92 in my pocket for four and a half months work. Wages at that time were $1.50 to $1.75 a day out of which we had to pay board.

In June 1909 I again struck out for work and started working on the section of the G.T.P. at Quinton. At that time the sections were long and ours stretched from half a mile west of Punnichy to one mile West of Raymore. I stayed until 30th November 1910 when I left for a visit to England. On my return to this country I had the opportunity to resume railroad work, as I was offered a section by Roadmaster Bob Johnson, but I turned it down for the homestead and a lifelong struggle with a mortgage.

Notes from Belle Patrick, Ernest's daughter-in-law

The Farrar family [Lizzie Farrar became Ernest's wife] had come to Canada from Manchester, England two years previously, and homesteaded between Bankend and Sheho.

Their place was known as 'Halfway House'. Many travellers, prospectors and homesteaders going either way would stop there to rest and feed their horses. No person left their home hungry, no matter what time of day or night a traveller would arrive.

The trend seemed to carry on, even since I came on this homestead. Many travellers and doctors would stop to rest and feed their horses, and have a warm drink, especially in the 1930s when we first had Municipal Doctors (Dr Little and Dr Polec). The roads were not good for cars and no snow ploughs.

In 1937 we had a terrible drought with a complete crop failure. 6th July, the same year, was a very hot day – 112 degrees Fahrenheit. Late in the afternoon, a black cloud appeared on the western horizon and a terrible twister passed through here. It intensified as it travelled eastward, leaving destruction in its path. Kelleher brick school and various other buildings were demolished. It stripped all the foliage off the trees and there was eight to ten inches of hail on the ground. It was said, one farmer and his wife were holding onto the door when the roof of the house disappeared!

There were no crops, hay or vegetables. The district was thankful to receive a carload of fruit and vegetables from Grand Forks, British Columbia for distribution.

In 1938 the horse disease known as encephalitis reached its epidemic stage during harvest and many horses died of the disease. That was the beginning of a new era – the change from horses to tractors.

That same year there was a caterpillar plague – millions of them crawling all over the fields and roads. Since there was no insecticide to destroy them, they stripped all the foliage off the trees.

Another change took place around here in the years 1941 – 1945: the change from threshing machines to combines. Since there was a scarcity of man labour during the war years, spiking and pitching of sheaves gave way to our present way of mechanical farming.

In the winter of 1947, our homestead saw its first bulldozer to clear the bush and the huge plough to break the land to make it available for farming.

In 1951 it rained nearly every day of harvest, resulting in the wheat sprouting in the swathes. It was difficult to harvest the crop and much of it was left out in the fields during the winter. The spring of 1952 brought very fine weather and in April the farmers were able to complete their fall harvest. In 1955 Saskatchewan Power expanded and into our district. Many poles were dug by hand and shovel.

My tribute to the pioneer:

'The courage and the hardship they endured, made it easier for us and a better way of life for our children.'

TO OLD TRAILS BY MRS BELLE PATRICK

I wonder if the road still winds
Past the old wooden bridge?
And do the willows twine above
The top of Farrar's ridge?
Do the trees in the summer time,
Shade Granny's road so well?
And do the cows in the field
Still come for evening bell?
I wonder if the rivers running yet
Past Harold's trodden well?
And do the roses grow their way
Still down the old trail hill?
I wonder, yes, I wonder,
About these things now past,
The joy of childhood summers
That went away so fast.

Petition for Organisation of School District

28th December 1917

Preliminary meeting

The number of acres of the accessible land in the proposed district is 11,516 acres. The number of children between the ages of five and sixteen years inclusive actually residing within the proposed district is 14. The total value of the assessable property within the proposed district is $39,600. A suitable site can be obtained at the centre of the district S.W. $^1/_4$ Sec. 9 Tp. 29 R. 14W2.

Organisation meeting held on 19th January 1918.

E. J. Ruxton, Chairman. Harry Beanland, Secretary. Milo Rockwell and Ernest Patrick, Trustees.

Ernest Patrick was appointed as a trustee. He also chose the name of the school, Allenby School, named after Edmund Allenby, Commander-in-Chief, Egyptian Expeditionary force in Palestine. During the First World War the late Field Marshall Allenby attracted much attention by his distinguished war service in Palestine.

The school was built in 1918 by Herman Collingwood, who had travelled to Canada on the same boat as Ernest Patrick and Arthur Wheeler. It was opened for introduction on 22nd July 1918.

Some statistics:

Miss Bessie Steele of Birch Creek in charge, salary $70 per month.

Janitor George Purdy, salary $2.00 per month.

One of the pupils received 50 cents a week for sweeping floors at the school.

A set of 20 Books of Knowledge was purchased at a cost of $49.00.

The school opened with five children, Elsie, Harry and Nellie Patrick and Isaac and Amos Thibault . By the end of the year there were 18 children.

Miss Steele rode horseback the nine miles to school each day and often gave Nellie (five years old) a ride with her. For the Patrick children it was a three mile walk each way.

In 1922 a teacherage was built in the school yard, and Mr D. L. Henkes, the first male teacher, and his wife lived there.

Elsie Patrick remembered one year, an early spring thaw followed by a hard frost, being able to walk on top of the snow straight across country, and getting to school in record time, being much shorter than the usual three miles. She also recalled walking to school in summer, each child carrying red lard pail containing their lunch. The same pails that Ernest used with salt in, as a treat for the cows, when he wanted to collect the herd together. When the cows spotted the children they would rush over and the children would have to hide in the hedge or bushes.

School Days of the Past by Margaret Keyowski (née Beanland), daughter of one of the original settlers

The children of today are very fortunate to have school buses to ride on and warm slacks or snowsuits to wear. We had to walk two miles, some had to walk further. There was no road, only what the horses and sleigh made, and when it blew in you had to walk through the deep snow. If someone happened to come along with a team and sleigh we sure appreciated it, although we were still cold. If it snowed overnight you had to make a fresh track with your feet. As a rule you left a little earlier, so you would not be late for school. There was no phone to tell your mother that you made it to school, and the same coming home at night. Your clothes consisted of long dresses, long coats and long stockings, which was not warm compared with the clothes of today. No hoods just toques and scarves. There was no such thing as slacks for the girls.

When the weather was a little warmer we used to pull a handmade sleigh to school, so at noon hour we could go sliding down a ravine $1/4$ east of Allenby School. We would hook all our sleighs together and make a train out of them to slide down this big hill. Sometimes things would go wrong and there would be a big pile up at the bottom of the hill, but no one would get seriously hurt, sometimes a few scratches and scrapes, and back we would go pulling our sleighs up the hill, so we could have another ride down.

On cold days the school was very cold, it had just a wood heater, and the wind would blow through the windows and doors. When it was about 30 degrees below the teacher would let us sit round the heater and do our work as it was too cold to sit at our desks. We usually had longer winter holidays and shorter summer ones, due to having to walk in the cold.

From 1919 to 1923 the Allenby Lodge of Saskatchewan Grain Growers Association held its meetings there. During those days the lodge organised the local picnics and sports days, baseball, football, tug of war, horse racing and even ladies hat trimming competitions for the men. It was amusing to see a group of men sitting on the ground with hats, feathers, flowers, ribbons and needle and thread putting together a glorious head piece which they had to wear. The horse races caused much excitement. These picnics were among the most successful and largest attended in the community.

The lodge was also responsible for many good concerts, pie and basket socials and old time dances in farm homes. The Allenby School Christmas concert became a well attended affair, as were all school concerts in those years. The pupils and teachers worked long hours in preparation. Mr E. Ruxton loaned his fine piano and assisted with his knowledge of musical training, which was much appreciated.

Arthur Wheeler's memories of the Old Homestead Days, beginning in 1906

I, with the late Ernie Patrick and Billy Lovell, left Portage La Prairie, on 10th April 1906 for Yorkton, and walked from there to Bank End, selected homesteads, and walked back to Yorkton and filed. We returned to Portage to work, then came back, walking out from Sheho on 18th October – returned to Sheho will Bill Hutchinson with oxen and wagon for winter supplies. Then on October 23rd commenced housekeeping.

An early settler in the Ladstock district was Frank Thibault. For many years he travelled far and wide preaching the gospel and holding services in railroad construction camps. He knew the Bible by heart, quoting any passage from memory. He was a very hospitable man, no person left his home hungry. No matter what time of day or night a visitor arrived, meat was put on the table. From him many of the homesteaders purchased horses, cattle, vegetables and meat etc. Horses were high in price $400 – $500 per team. Oxen could be purchased for $35 or $40 each.

Another old timer was Charlie Wright from Manchester, England, known for his speed digging wells and stooking. He could dig a 4 foot well 14 feet deep in one day. He stooked 600 acres of wheat (1,000 lbs twine) in 14 days wages 40 cents an acre, finishing one day after the binders.

Another homesteader who came in 1906 was Captain E. Ruxton, a Liverpool man who saw the world in sailing ships. He went one day to Lipton with oxen to get a piano and other goods, probably the first piano in the district. As a consequence his house became the social centre for some time. By the time he reached Lipton he had had enough of oxen and traded them for a team of horses.

Mr Ruxton's neighbours were Alf and Ruby Chopping. Alf was a racing cyclist and cabinet maker by trade. A skilled craftsman he built one of the finest dove-tailed log buildings in the district. A neighbour asked him to repair a broken fiddle and the repair could never be detected.

On one occasion, running short of provisions, Alf decided to go to the store on Round Plains. He hooked up the oxen to the stone-boat, on which he fastened two kitchen chairs, and away he and his wife went on a fine summer day. On the trail home, plagued by mosquitoes and other troubles a neighbour was alerted by much swearing and shouting. When the neighbour reached the top of the hill he saw Alf and Ruby sitting in their chairs atop the stone-boat in the middle of the slough – the oxen very comfortable with the water up to their backs, swishing their tails and giving Alf and Ruby a shower bath.

Walter Sox, another bachelor, practiced for a short while as a Veterinary Surgeon. One night in the winter we attended a stag party there, mostly bachelors. Tom and Sam Folster were the fiddlers. During the evening Walter had a huge pot on the stove steaming away. About midnight he hoisted a big plum pudding out, and that comprised our supper. It was good but took us all our time to clean it up.

Mr and Mrs Purdy lived opposite the school and were always interested in school activities. I well remember seeing Mr Purdy seed a small field by hand. He was an expert at broadcasting. Probably the last time it was done in this district. Mr and Mrs Purdy can claim to something of a record in that their 11 children attended Allenby School the period extending from the opening in 1918 until 1951.

Milo Rockwell was one of the first to operate a S.P. stream threshing outfit in the district, and for many years had long runs. Sometimes until Christmas. He often had difficulty moving the big outfit across low places and creeks. In 1911 and 1912 wood had to be used for burning as the straw was too wet. In 1912 he finished his run on Ernest Patrick's farm on December 30th. Later he introduced the wing feeder to speed up operations. He covered a wide area as there were only a few outfits at that time. On 6th December 1911 Ed Landry drove four horses on a snow plough to break a road to enable the machine to move. It was in 1913 that threshing was first done by gasoline power.

Pat Thorpe, a well known character built many shacks for homesteaders. Usually they were 14 feet by 16 feet of hewed logs, half inch boards, tar paper and again half inch boards, one window and door. Pat cut the logs, hewed, and did all the work (the homesteader providing the lumber and window) for $40 each. He usually selected the site, one from which the homesteader could overlook most of his domain. He could neither read nor write, but could sing songs – all day long to the same tune, relating to incidents of the trail, the voyageurs and lumberjacks.

It was Isaac Pickering who put up a stake with an old boot on top, at a fork in the trails to guide settlers freighting goods from Sheho to the west. This was long known as The Old Boot Trail.

Mrs Bonner was known far and wide as the maternity nurse in the days of no doctors and no hospitals. Whenever a call came she was always ready and willing.

As a further illustration of the lack of medical services Charlie Wright told me that around 1906 he used to drive a livery team out of Yorkton. on one occasion he drove Dr Polac to a rancher's home north if Sheho a distance of 68 miles and back in one day. This was in subzero weather and in an open cutter. On going to bed he was roused two hours later, and with another team drove the doctor to another home 50 miles east of Yorkton. Charlie's clothing consisted of woollen underwear, two suits of chamois cloth pants, mackinaw pants, overalls and a sheepskin coat. Still it was very cold on long distances except for the warmth derived from a bottle usually carried. Pay was $65.00 a month out of which board had to be paid. Except for a few spots, the grade of the G.T.P. Railway was completed on 14th November 1907.

On 21st January 1908 I went to a barn dance at Kelleher to celebrate the arrival of the first train, a work train. It was on 23rd September 1908 that the first passenger train carrying executives travelled over this railroad westward.

We used the telephone for the first time on 11th December 1912. In 1917 the Elfros telephone line was constructed.

22nd May 1910, first saw Haley's Comet.

July 1922 attended a Chatauqua in Leross, attended by Mrs Pankhurst the noted British Suffragette leader, who gave an address. This was the last of the Chatauquas, which brought first class entertainment to country districts.

1927 C.P.R. started construction of branch line Foam Lake to Wishart.

1928 Steel laid, and first grain delivered to Bank End this year.

Now looking back and making comparisons, the early days of settlement were good days and unspoiled. Countryside – plenty of wild life and a wonderful spirit of co-operation in work and play. Money did not seem to be the prime consideration. Yet people managed to get along without much. Today when the young generation ask why the old folks held on in spite of difficulties and poor returns, it is difficult to give a true answer. And so we leave the early days and scenes which can never be recaptured except by the memories of those who took part.

Arthur J. Wheeler
14th April 1952
Bank End, Sask

Lightning Source UK Ltd.
Milton Keynes UK
UKOW052046170712

196143UK00003B/13/P